Kangaroos in Delco

It's kinda rare to see a kan. field these days. But there he is hopping down the hill and staring me in the eyes. I pulled over. Tried to video him but he wanted no parts of being recorded at that time. I posted it on FB instead. I did that because many people tend to think I'm drinking when I post. I wasn't drinking and I'm not crazy.

When the next passenger got in, I told her about the kangaroo. My initial thoughts were that this lady is going to think I'm a weirdo and jump out of the car. Instead, she replied "Everybody knows about that kangaroo. It is an injured deer that gets around on its hind legs. The deer injured itself trying to get over the Holy Cross Cemetery fence". Adding that in the comments on Facebook saved me a little face. Except for my friend's daughter, who also happens to have a kangaroo tattooed on her arm. To this day she still slips something onto my FB wall about a kangaroo. Bet she still thinks I was drinking. I don't and never did drink but I'm not putting her name out there. She may unfriend me.

Trend Setter

I've been doing ridesharing since before ridesharing became fashionable. Shortly after the age of sixteen, I fell in love with cars. Anything that I could get my hands on for under $500. Had them all. Ford Mustang, Chevy Camaro, Pontiac Trans Am, Plymouth Barracuda, and a jalopy of a Chevy Belair

I painted the Belair with a roller and brush. The winds of highway I-95 blew it off in sheets while driving down the road. Painted everything: The seats, dashboard, and even the steering wheel.

The rear wheels fell off the Camaro. Cut the wheel well out with a pair of tin snips, threw a set of sixty mag wheels on, along with a pair of struts. Beautiful. Only mistake was forgetting to tighten the lug nuts before going on interstate 95. Whoops.

The Pontiac never needed oil. So, I thought. Blew a rod on that baby. The Mustang and Barracuda were only decoys to attract women. That never worked out so well anyway.

Ride Captain Ride

Ride, captain ride upon your mystery ship. Be amazed at the friends you have here on your trip. The first "unofficial" ride came after stopping at a Seven Eleven at night. Girl said her name was Heather. Cute little thing. Five feet tall. She asked me for a ride as I came out of the convenience store. I was eating a hotdog and chugging down something to drink in the other hand. How could I resist?

Cruised Heather all over the place that night. Later learned that wasn't her real name. Stopped anywhere she wanted before taking her to an old theatre on South Street. She asked if I wanted to go in and see a concert with her and that she was going to flip the bill. Upon arriving, she took me down a dark alley and banged on the back door of the theatre. A few guys opened the door and she slithered in and left me standing at the back door to a very loud slamming noise. I knocked forever and the guards opened the door and said, "Get Lost". "Heather" was the lead singer of a popular band called Pretty Poison.

Driving home on a flat tire was no fun. The consolation prize was being able to have had a lot of kisses from the Lead singer of Pretty Poison that night. Fun. But let me tell you about the rides that put a little cash in the pockets:

The Kiss That Pays

12:30am pickup at Barnaby's in Ridley park. Two girls. One's celebrating her 23rd birthday. Birthday girl decides she wants a birthday kiss. I laugh and tell her I'm old enough to be her dad. When we arrive, I get her overnight bag out of the trunk. She demands the kiss and plants one in a surprise attack. Somebody just got paid for a kiss. She chases me around the car and tells me she wants to make out. I escape. 6:30am I get another ping. Guess who? I'm thinking she's sobered up and accept her ride request. First thing she says to me is "I'm getting myself a REAL kiss this time"! I look at the app. She's going home to Conshohocken. Great! That gives me 23 minutes to convince her along the ride that I'm not the one for her cause I have some serious issues. Upon arriving, she said "Nice try. Pucker up buttercup".

All that effort for nothing. Then she says "You're strange. But don't change". And I let her.

I let her get her bags out of the trunk by herself. That's what I let her.

Well, Hello There

My name is Bill McHugh. I've been called worse. I've been called better. Driving for Uber was the side hustle. It allowed me to maintain my full-time business and gave me the flexibility to take care of my father. He passed February 2017. I live to laugh, work hard, and continue to struggle like everybody else. We can't please everybody all the time. Oh… but I could. My rating was the highest in the state of Pennsylvania. I've been threatened, seduced, propositioned, and a whole lot of other things. Along the way, I've met 10,000 of the most unusual, entertaining people imaginable. People like you. The people and situations I've encountered as a driver have changed my perspective on life. Most rides came late at night. Lieutenant Joe Kendra used to say that nothing good happens after midnight. These stories are for your entertainment. They are to enlighten people of what goes on in the world of Ridesharing. Thank you, Uber, for allowing me to become a PASSENGER IN THE LIVES OF OTHERS. I hope you all enjoy this ride.

Reason for the Season

Both of my parents had been sick for several years and had moved in with my wife and I for several reasons. For them, it was beneficial as they got older and required more help with their health. For my wife, it was an extra set of hands on the kitchen stove and some supplemental income.

For me, it was more conversation and a way to thank my parents for a good upbringing. I grew up in the lower middle-class neighborhood of Sharon Hill. My dad was a cement finisher who liked to drink when he was younger. My mom was a working mother. She and my father managed to do the best they could with what little they had. That was more than enough for me. Owning a consulting company gave me a lot of flexibility to take care of my sick parents. It also gave me the flexibility to start driving for Uber when I had the chance. Driving has always been a relaxing thing and I wanted to parlay it into some supplemental cash. Uber did the background check and I was on the road within hours.

My first ride was in Southwest Philadelphia. That was the neighborhood my wife grew up in that had changed in the past twenty years. The first rider was a cleaning lady. She filled the trunk with all kinds of cleaning supplies including mops and brooms. Good time to mention that her mop destroyed my peanut butter Kandy Cakes.

The ride took me deeper into rougher neighborhoods. The conversation was limited because I was nervous, and she had a thick accent from Jamaica. The money came to around $8. Nothing exciting but it pinged for a second ride. Can't remember who or where but at the end of that first Sunday I made somewhere around $59 in over two hours. There were between five and eight rides. Couldn't wait to go home and brag about the extra bucks I made on a boring Sunday afternoon.

There were troubles learning the app. Most drivers were using mounted phones. I was using an iPad because I was too lazy to get a pair of reading glasses and couldn't see the print on a phone. The riders, at this point, had a leg up on their driver. They knew the ins and outs and knew how to play the game.

Help! I Need Somebody

A sixteen-year-old kid shouts "Uber" and jumps in the front seat of my car. I just dropped a woman off at Walmart. I said to the kid "Get out. You gotta have the app". He replies "Please, Mister. I'm only going six blocks. I will give you my Obama Phone.

I'm playing the world's smallest violin: (Help) I need somebody. (Help) Not just anybody. (Help) You know I need someone. Help me get my feet back on the ground.

"Please, Mister", the kid pleaded. I felt bad for that kid. He was nice enough and I tell him to get in and keep his Obama phone. He insisted that I keep the phone because he got himself a real phone and was working at Walmart. He said he doesn't need no Obama phone, anymore. Thanks Kid! Wish he only knew what became of that phone in a later story.

The Monkeys

Many riders acted like monkeys. And people say we monkey around. But we're too busy driving to put anybody down. Hey, hey we're the monkeys.

Monkey see, monkey do. That's exactly what the next girl did. She lived on the previous rider's block. She also attempted the same trick he pulled. "Uber", she yelled. Then she just climbed into the car like a monkey. There was no ping. She didn't have an Obama Phone to offer. Booted her. That trick wasn't going to work again.

Sundays would never be the same. I hustled. And hustled. Those initial rides were fun but they were dangerously close to Kensington.

Welcome to The Jungle

Welcome to the jungle. We've got fun and games. I'd heard Kensington was a rough place ridden with drugs and prostitutes. I never encountered it in the few brief times I drove thru there. I do remember taking my mother in law thru there when we diverted off I-95 in the snowstorm. I only remember it looking dilapidated back then. I don't remember it being a war zone or a third world country. and many of the houses appeared run down.

Accidental Rider

Had an early morning ride that cancelled as I was nearing the address. It was also a Sunday morning. Early. Like around 7:00am or 8:00am. I saw a girl approaching the corner and pulled over to ask her if she was the Uber rider who cancelled. I don't remember what she said but somehow ended up asking her if she was ok. She asked if I wanted a date.

Her name was Megan. I didn't think she could have been a prostitute. I had only talked to her for a few mins about what was going on. Shortly after, Megan got into the car and I took her to a Dunkin Donuts on Erie Ave and had a long conversation with her. Megan said she was on her way to work but had run into some "complications" and financial issues. I told her she didn't look like the type to be struggling. There had to be something I could do to help this woman without putting me in the path of harm's way. She appeared honest enough.

I didn't need ridesharing to learn that. Forget my family's medical struggles. Forget the merchants that harassed me every waking minute of the day. I'd had my own struggles unrelated to drugs or alcohol since the beginning of time in one way or another.

Ridesharing was a friendly reminder that the rest of the world had their own struggles. I didn't earn much on those rides that Sunday morning and was damned if I was going to blow it on a stranger. A cheap one-dollar breakfast at Dunkin Donuts had to suffice.

After out nice talk, she said she wanted help. That was a reoccurring theme with everybody. The difference most of the time was that they want help but were never willing to get help. There is nothing anybody can do to help anybody unless the person is willing to help themselves. They need to put both feet in the water. Can't tell you how many times people would drum that into my head, yet I'd be the one thinking a miracle would happen.

Pharmaceutical Assistance

I offered to help her as best I could. I mentioned I had a friend I could call who owned a pharmacy in Folcroft and that he could help or offer us some advice. When I called Brian, he said to take the girl to a hospital. The first hospital that came to mind was Fitzgerald Mercy Hospital. It was on the way home and I wouldn't have to venture all thru the city looking for a hospital that had no parking.

Sometime along the way, Megan said she needed to stop home first to feed her dog before she went to the hospital. Home was at the intersection of Jasper and Venango.   I agreed to wait outside while she fed the dog and said goodbye to her "father". Little did I know her "father" was actually her Sugar Daddy and "home" meant a place to get her drugs. Along the way to the hospital Megan appeared to be getting very tired. I had a hard time understanding her words and called my friend Brian who advised me she was high.

Full panic mode had set in. Brian told me to stop by his pharmacy. The girl had told me she never used a needle and only took pills to make her more relaxed. When we arrived, Brian and his staff came out to the car and brought her into the pharmacy. Brian, while carrying this woman, felt a bump on the back of the pretty girl's neck. "Right here, Bill. That's where she shot up. She's a junkie. Take her to the hospital and leave her there."

There was no way was I going to put a stranger back into my car who had done drugs and appeared to be dying. He called in a Narcan shot via her insurance and told me to drive as fast as I can. I

7

could get her to the hospital faster than an ambulance could. My left hand held the wheel and my right hand held the Narcan. Both hands were shaking all the way to the hospital. I thought the girl was going to die.

Instead of leaving the girl at the hospital, I waited for her. The hospital said her vitals were stable and recommended a treatment program. I wanted to get the girl help so back to Kensington to get her belongings at the same house. She went in the front door and out the back. I watched her go back down an alley and couldn't believe it. Not sure if I was more shocked or more pissed off. Never was I going back to Kensington.

That was the first ridesharing story that went onto Facebook. Two weeks later, a friend posted a comment that many people had overdosed in Kensington. They were all on that block. The article showed a picture of a redheaded woman in a black leather jacket. It was – or so I thought – the same woman who was in my car that day. It was an upsetting event and promised myself I would never take another ride to Kensington. The problem with ridesharing is that you, as a driver, do not have the ability to control where people are going.

All rides seemed to go to Kensington. Gentrification. Had no idea what that word meant. So much of that area had been re-developed. The younger generation were going there to places like The Garage and Frankford Hall. Those people tipped. I loved it. Problem was, go a few blocks East, West, North or South and you were right there in the bad lands.

We've Gotta Get Out of This Place

In this dirty old part of the city where the sun refused to shine. People tell me there ain't no use in tryin'.

Now my girl you're so young and pretty. And one thing I know is true. You'll be dead before your time is due, I know.

It's 3am and I'm sitting at a traffic light on Kensington and

Lehigh Ave. Beside me is a cop. I see a guy climb a tree and smash a window into an abandoned house. I point it out to the cop who advised me to let it go. The officer calls the man down out of the tree. She was the he that climbed the tree and broke into that abando that night at 3am. That rhyme was coincidental, so you know. Honestly. She was beautiful. Couldn't believe that a thirty-two-year-old woman with an eighteen-month-old baby was homeless. Most people knew her as Star. Her real name was Candice. The father of the baby was somebody referred to as a "John". She had met him while working the streets. He owned a home. She didn't. I will never know if it was her husband or the father of the baby. She had her issues, too.

I called my wife asking if I could put her up in a hotel for the night until the woman figured something out. I had no idea that she could have stolen the television, trashed the hotel or – worse – robbed or set me up. She wanted to make sure that I come back and pick her up in the morning. She would need to go back to Kensington for her drugs or she would get sick.

I jumped on the opportunity because I believed I could talk her into getting help. The next day on the ride back, she told me she wasn't ready for help. She also said she had Aids. Looking at her, one would never know that. I was in disbelief that she was out there doing dates while she was suffering from Aids. She said to me "Bill, eighty five percent of us have Aids, Hep C, or some other diseases. The other fifteen percent lie about it or don't know".

I said to her I couldn't believe it. While looking around at the other girls that morning, I asked her "What about her? And her? And her"? Star said, "Every one of them". I shook my head in disbelief. Star called one of the girls over. Her name was Jessica.

Star said to Jessica, "tell him what you have". Jess said "Nothing. Want to do a date". Star went nuts. Pretty as she was, she was also tough. The undisputed leader of that area who had been out there for over fifteen years. Everybody knew Star.

Star told me that back in the day, she was a high paid call girl living everywhere from NY to Vegas. Heavy drug usage reduced Star to a homeless girl living on the streets of Kensington. Something about her made me want to help her. Every single day for two weeks my day would start in Kensington on that corner of Kensington and Lehigh. I'd bring Star a cup of coffee or hot chocolate. No money. A warm drink and a lot of persuasion.

Knocking on Heaven's Door

I learned a lot from Star. She never knew it but our talks were actually counseling for a guy who didn't know he needed counseling. With her and her "friends", I could talk about anything. Who were they to judge? They made me feel comfortable talking about anything. I loved our conversations and the conversations with her "friends".

Star finally was ready to go to rehab. She said "Bill, pick me up tomorrow and take me to rehab. I want to live". I flew out of there all excited and went and spent hours upon hours at Fitzgerald Hospital with my dad. He hadn't been doing too well but the staff assured me to "Go home and get some rest".

Watch my daddy in bed a-dyin'. Watched his hair been turnin' grey. He's been workin' and slavin' his life away. I know he's been workin' so hard.

I bee-lined back to Kensington to take Star to rehab. No sooner did I pull up to the curb only to witness an ambulance on the corner. Her lifeless body laying across the intersection. The hospital called. My father also passed.

You can't make this stuff up. From that moment on, I wanted to play Captain-Save-a-Hoe. We gotta get out of this place. If it's the last thing we ever do. We gotta get out of this place. Girl, there's a better life for me and you.

I wanted to save every single one of those beautiful girls who were struggling. In hindsight, The Kensington addicts were an escape from the loss of my father. People grieve in different ways.

All I could manage to do was try to console my mom and stay busy to prevent a meltdown. And so, the journey began.

Who's Afraid of Who

After Star's passing, there was a girl who I used to see while bringing Star something warm to drink. Jessica was one of the girls Star called over and asked to disclose what diseases were out there on the streets. Jessica claimed not to have any diseases. She was looking for business. Star forced her to be honest. Jessica didn't have to admit anything, but she did. Maybe it was the persuasion of Star. Maybe it was a girl who was struggling being honest. Neither mattered.

A few times I had asked Jessica to get herself some help. She was never ready. Flash forward many months and I had taken my last ridesharing trip of the night. It ended up on Whitaker Ave in Phila north of the badlands. It was 3am and as I pulled up to the McDonalds drive thru to order a drink, the lights went out at McDonalds. I can still hear the "poof" sound that the lights made.

McDonalds was closed. There was a woman cowering beside the dumpster several feet away. I don't know who was more afraid of who – Me of her or her of me. Veering the car off to the left, I approached the woman and asked if she was ok. She answered that she was okay, but her feet were cold. There were no shoes on this woman and the clothing she had weren't enough to even break the wind. The wind was blowing out of the east that night. I barely was able to recognize the woman as one of the people who used to be on the corner with Star.

The woman was Jessica. She had shed a few pounds. Her hair was a mess. Her voice sounded nothing like I remembered it to be that night in Kensington. We talked.

The first thing I did was to comfort Jessica. She was not comprehensive enough to even worry if I was an undercover cop or a John looking for a date. The conversation started the usual way: "So where did it all go wrong, Jessica? Do you remember me"? She nodded her head although I am sure she had no idea I who I was. Again, I asked her where it all went wrong.

Jessica said that she was ok. The reason she was out there that night was to earn a few bucks so she could put food on her father's plate. She admitted being homeless but did seem to prioritize getting food. Not for her father or her own wellbeing. I went on to ask her to tell me a little more about her father. Where was he, etc.

Jessica told me that her father lived in the basement of a house in Upper Darby with his brother. There was no room for her. She would often enter thru the basement window to leave food and a little cash for her father. As hard as that was to believe, I gave her the benefit of the doubt. I assured her that I could get her in to his house that night.

She agreed to take the ride to Upper Darby. She was out of options for the night and it was a warm car for however long it took to get down to Upper Darby. The trip took what seemed like forty-five minutes or so. Of course, I bombed Jessica with questions all the way down.

Jessica had a story to tell that was one of the crazier stories I had heard. Early on, I was very naive to stories people would tell. I would believe anything and everything a rider would tell me. Jessica's story blew my mind.

Storied Past

At the age of seven, she watched her mom get executed in the head in South Philadelphia. Her mom was slated to go to trial as a witness in a famous case from the seventies. She was sitting on her mon's lap at the time of the execution. Her cousin Amy had a tragic incident that made national news. Amy was abducted on the highway coming home from a club on Lancaster Avenue one night. I knew Amy as well. Her family frequented a drive thru dairy store that I managed years ago. The incident with Jessica's mother being executed was enough to ruin any child's life. She was sitting on her mom's lap at the time.

Everything was closed at that time of the morning when I drove her to Upper Darby. There were no stops along the way. Jessica only had a brown paper bag with her containing her clothes and who knows what else. We pull up. She bangs on the window. Her father comes out.

It was then that I remembered the Obama phone that the teenage rider insisted I take. I told Jessica she would need the phone more than I would and handed it to her as she got out. Boy, did that phone play an important role. The next morning, I woke up and found everything Jessica owned was still sitting in that brown paper bag. She'd left it in my trunk.

Forgetting about the phone, I drove back to Upper Darby. Her father came out and said the "piece of garbage" was back out on the street. Speaking of garbage, he refused to take her belongings when I tried to give them to her. What kind of man would do that to his daughter?

Then I remembered the Obama phone. For three days, it went to voicemail. No answer then straight to voicemail. On the last attempt, she answered in a slurred voice. "Jessica, it's me. Bill. The Uber Driver". Jessica was thrilled when I told her I had her belongings. She asked me to drop them off to her back on Lehigh Avenue in Kensington. That was around 7:00pm on a Saturday night. The money night.

There was no way I wanted to sacrifice my money night bringing clothes to struggling addicts. in Kensington no less. Realizing it would be the last chance I had to get her belongs back to her, onward I went. Jessica was there sitting on the corner with two other women. All three of them were impaired. They had over a lot of dope between them but, were willing to go to a crisis center. The tall woman dumped their dope out. I insisted, they weren't getting in my car with it and I wasn't going to wait another second for them.

The tall girl said to go to Charter Fairmount in Roxboro. I

followed her advice, not knowing anywhere else to take them. The tall women later told me she only went for the ride to make sure Jessica got there. The third woman disappeared as soon as we arrived. The intelligent woman had a home, an education, and a family who cared. She lived in the Fishtown section of Philadelphia and made a lot of money. For her, heavy usage was a thing of her past. She told me she went down to Kensington on a rare occasion. She considered herself a "recreational" user. I don't believe there is such thing as a "recreational" user but that's my opinion.

Jessica called me several months later. She said she wasn't going to make it and wanted a hug. Her weight was down to eighty pounds. Jessica passed away two days later at the same corner where I met her to give her the hug. She was the second of what would be more than a dozen addicts to pass that were given a ride to rehab.

Peanut Butter & Jelly

Any mother may be able to relate to this. My rider and I somehow ended up behind a school bus. You know how I love those school buses. The rider is on her way to work early in the morning. We see some grapes fly out the rear side window of the bus. I'm thinking LITTERBUG. The rider mumbles "unbelievable". Then a container of milk goes out the window of the bus. I said to my rider "look at those little brats littering". The rider seems to agree.

Finally, a PB & J sandwich goes out the window. At that point, my rider yells "stop this car! I'm gonna kill him. He's throwing his lunch out the window again". The kid was hers. He found something better to eat on the bus. Can't we all remember the days of trading our healthy lunches for anything containing sugar? Our poor moms. Guess that's a part of growing up – except I never completely did grow up. Does anybody have any sugar wafers they'd like to barter with an ex Uber Driver?

Supermarket Ride

I'm shopping in a local supermarket. A guy is begging for money up and down the aisles. He's young and healthy enough to work. He won't go away. I report him to the manager. He's escorted out.

Now he's standing out front doing the same thing. I may be bald but I'm having a bad hair day. Wasn't in the mood to be hassled by a panhandler. We exchange a few words. I tell him I am a ridesharing driver and offer to take him to look for a job.

No sooner do I get the groceries in the car and I get a ping. It's him. Guess I was the closet driver to that supermarket. I accept the ride. "Can you take me to get a job", he asks.

Long story short, the man is now working. We went to a steak shop down the street that I had a relationship with, and they hired the man. I see him from time to time. He was a good man in a bad position. It felt good to help somebody in need.

Smash and Run

A regular rider gets in and says "Did you have a normal, crazy weekend, Bill? Saturday night I was in an Uber pool going to a restaurant in South Philadelphia. Two other girls get in and are headed to the same restaurant to pick up food they ordered. By the time we arrive, the restaurant had already closed. The two girls got out and smashed the window to the restaurant then jumped back into the Uber and told the driver to GO! GO! GO! So that was my Saturday night date with the cops and a few lunatics".

Simple Simons

What are the chances of three riders in a row named Simon? The first was a woman. That ride went well. The next ping is also for a Simon. I get to the Villanova Campus and two groups of people approach the car at the same time and don't know each other. All of us are shocked. I'm thinking somebody is playing a game on me.

We sort it out. Both Simons had ordered an Uber and were going to two different places. It turned out that the second Simon wasn't waiting on a white Prius. He was going to Center City. Luckily, the Simon who went with me was going to Collegeville along with her friend. Ca Ching! Big bucks for that ride with the surge and distance. Can there be four people in the world named Simon who Uber? Sure was. The fourth Simon is a story of its own and coming later.

Mistakes

We all make them. Pick up this school teacher on her way to work. Enjoying a great conversation with her. Miss a few exits. You know how that goes. Accidentally go over the Ben Franklin Bridge instead of getting off in the city. She says, "Don't worry about it". I say "Can you believe that Uber app? It does that all the time".

We keep going. And going. Up interstate 76. Whoops. She's already late. I tell her I will shut the app off, so she doesn't get charged for the additional time and distance but forget to shut it off. Forty-five minutes later, she arrives at school. She got a complete and unsolicited tour of the city, I apologize for "Uber's App's mistakes.

I never understood how Uber could charge a woman so much money for what should have been a six-minute ride. She even left a sweet tip for the Uber Driver thinking Uber would refund that astronomical fee. It never came off my end. How nice! What a Sweetheart! LOL

Audi Five

First noticed this Audi 500 around December of 2017. Less than 2 years old, loaded, tinted windows. It was blacker than black with a thick coating of dust all over the car. It's been tagged

"Abandoned" by the proper authorities but hasn't been towed or removed in over 5 months.

The luxurious car is sitting in a National wildlife preserve. The park is frequented by a gabillion tourists. Tags are expired. Inspection is expired. Etc. May I mention that preserve often serves as an outdoor restroom for many divers? Now, I'm not about to incriminate myself that one. Not sure why I even brought that up. Anyway, who can afford not to have their Audi for all those months?

Threw a pic of the Audi on Facebook. That was pretty much an invitation for anybody to come get the car – legally or not. Was told it may have been a bait car. Was also told it may have been stolen. Was told it may contain a dead body or two in the trunk, etc. Who knows? Anyway, shortly after that post, the Audi was gone. Coincidental? Not! Had at least 10 people – women no less – claiming the car was now being stored in their garage. For a while there, the girl with the tattoo of a kangaroo on her arm would post something about her newfound Audi.

You're sick. Get out!

Sick riders brought and instant fear and phobia. Having driven enough sick riders builds one's immune system up pretty good. A man named John and his friend got into my car. They both had the flu. John, in between coughs and sneezes, says "Thank you for picking us up. Thank you! Thank you! His DNA was flying all over the car. I told John there was no need for a thank you. That's what we do. We're Uber Drivers.

John replied "You don't understand. The last driver threw us out when he heard us sneezing. Before he did, he asked if my name was John. When I replied "yes" he said we got in the wrong car and that another driver was on his way. John said the Uber driver sped away like a bat out of hell. John said figured out that the man didn't want him in his car while he was sick. His friend said to John "Wait a minute. How did he know your name was John"?

Goes to show, not all Uber drivers are compassionate.

People Are Strange

People are strange when you're a stranger. Faces look ugly when you're strange. Streets are uneven when you're down. Faces come out of the rain when you're strange. No one remembers your name.

Uber pools were challenging to say the least. Scratch that. They were nightmares! After an attitude adjustment, I later referred to the pools as my "Party Rides". I learned to play the role of matchmaker and headhunter by interacting with riders. Pool rides combined complete strangers heading to the same vicinity. I could write another book on the Uber pools alone. Imagine how difficult it was to get said strangers to agree on a radio station. They also had to agree on the temperature settings and the content of conversation. Not easy. On this pool, I had a feeling it was going to be a load of trouble. And it was.

The first woman "Goth Girl" was coming from a bar. The next two riders aka "Coyotes" getting in the car were 2 guys who couldn't hook up with anybody earlier in the night. Mix in the last girl – "Perfume Lady". She worked at Sephora on Chestnut Street in Philadelphia and we've got ourselves a ride. Perfume lady required a call to inform her that we had been sitting there waiting. It felt like…forever. When I called her, I accidentally put the woman on speaker phone.

The other riders were shouting "she sounds like a bitch. Leave her there". I thought about doing that because she had an attitude from Jump Street. I didn't want her killing my perfect Uber rating. Nevertheless, I let her in the car. Boy was she pissed off! She was mad at the comments the others made about her when she was on speaker phone. She was more pissed because the Coyotes in the back made her ride BETWEEN them rather than giving her the end seat. Goth Girl in the front didn't like a thing about Perfume lady. She was more relentless than the Coyotes and criticized everything. From the way Perfume lady dressed to her lifestyle. To her overwhelmingly strong odor of... Perfume.

Somehow, the conversation changed into an argument. It was about whoever was paying higher utility bills at their abodes. Guess who egged that conversation on? That was an effort to divert the negative conversation that was transpiring? Those who know me know I am an analytical person. After each trip, I always wondered what I could have or should have done. It didn't matter at this point. The catfight was underway.

The coyotes refused to get out of the car when we reached their destination. They were enjoying every second of the girls arguing and were willing to pay to stay in the car. They weren't going to hook up with anybody anyway that night, remember? Goth girl had me to drop her off in an alley before she "killed the bitch". After I dropped her off in the alley, the coyotes asked to be dropped off several feet later. They wanted to hunt down the Goth lady like a wild pack that they were. The Perfume girl insisted I drop her off in that alley as well because she still wanted a piece of the Goth Girl.

Oh, how I wanted to get out myself and watch that carnival. PING. Another ride. Darn! Told myself to never allow future riders to discuss their utility bills with each other. The rest of my Ubering career would go smooth. Right? Wrong!

A Hoagie! I'm Eatin' It!

It's roughly 2:40am. A local popular watering hole named Barnaby's has long since closed but there is one last ride coming out of there. I picked up a husband and his wife. He was about 6'4" with a thick Irish Bode. His wife was much younger and quite attractive. I'm 5'11". The husband was in the back seat. The wife was sitting beside me in the front seat.

The drunken man thought his wife was flirting with me. He started slapping his wife, punching her, and pulling her hair. What's one to do at that time in the morning with a drunken monster in the back seat and he is bigger that you? By the time I called 911, it would have been a full-blown disastrous incident. It wasn't a short ride, either, considering they were going from Barnaby's in Havertown to West Chester. That's a forty-minute ride.

After mustering up a little courage, I reached into the back and grabbed the man's wrist. Told him if he touched her again, it would be his last bad move of the night. Well, his wife went nuts. It's everything you see on the television show Cops. The woman attacked me and shouted "That's my husband! He's attacking me, too. I still may have her teeth marks embedded in my arm. The marks also may have come from another rider on a different trip. Many times, I felt we should have received Combat pay.

Along the way, we stopped at a Wawa. My chance to lose them both, but she doesn't get out of the car. He goes into to use the bathroom but comes out with a hoagie. Before he staggered over to the car, I gave his wife two choices: Either get out with her husband or go home without him. As her husband approached, she said "GO. GO. GO"! Away we went.

He may have been drunk but the husband had pretty good aim tossing the hoagie in the rear window. His words were hard to decipher as we sped off and left him there. Some, in part, because of all the alcohol he'd consumed. More, in part, because of that thick Irish bode. It may have been a cheap hoagie, but it went on to become paradise for the next set of drunken riders.

The hoagie never made it into their house. My fault. I was so anxious to get rid of her, that I forgot about the hoagie in the back seat. Chalked that one up to memory loss. The next set of drunken riders got in the car and one of them sat on the hoagie and said "A hoagie! I'm eatin' it"! Not only was that funny, but it was poetic justice: No hoagie for the wife abuser.

Oh, No. Not Again

The guy who ordered that ride and who sat on the hoagie was also smashed. Poor guy didn't have a chance to eat the hoagie because he was passed out within a minute of sitting on it. His two friends weren't far behind him when it comes to sobriety. Took them on a long ride from West Chester to Northeast Philadelphia.

When we arrived, the guy who ordered the ride was still passed out. We had to carry him up two flights of stairs. His buddy said he wasn't going into his friend's pocket to get the guy's keys. We propped him up against the railing and left him there. I had a guilt trip about the guy freezing to death or falling down the steps, so I asked one of his friends to call the guy's wife.

All the lights go on in the house and I hear her screaming into the phone "not again". We went to help her get him into the house and he wakes up and jumps into his SUV. I Thought he was going to drive away and hurt himself or somebody else, so I blocked him in with my Prius. He hits the garage remote in his SUV and screams "Who are you? Who are you"? The garage opens two feet and the man crawled in and closed the door. Mission accomplished.

Barnaby's Fire

It is my belief that the drunken couple were the cause of the notorious Barnaby's Fire in Havertown. The couple appeared to be the last to leave Barnaby's that night. As I pulled up, I remember the man smoking like a chimney and thinking this man was going to stink up my car. It was the onset of spring and the weather had been nice enough for landscapers to come out and plant a few flowers.

Besides, that night was quite cold. Before the guy got into the car, he tossed his cigarette into a flowerbed at Barnaby's. The flowerbed had been mulched earlier in the day. I ditched the drunken man at the Wawa and took his wife home alone, as mentioned. While driving the drunks back to Northeast Philadelphia, Barnaby's was ablaze. People surmised that it was the owners who started that fire for insurance purposes. Speculation, people. You know who I think started that fire.

Return Policy

The following Sunday, I pick up one of the friendliest of guys I've had in a while. He was headed from Norwood to his girlfriend's house in New Jersey. The friendly rider wanted to stop at a Kmart first. The reason for the stop was to return his wife's angels before he went over to New Jersey. Yep. I said his wife's angels. Emphasis on wife. He claimed his neighbor was kind enough to store the angels in his garage for a few days. Then other neighbors started complaining about the noise they were making. The man claimed the police were called and he was told to get his wife's angels out of his neighbor's garage.

The man was tired of his wife's angels causing troubles around in their marriage. If such angels did exist, one must wonder if they were what was causing the man's issues at home. Couldn't have anything to do with him having a girlfriend on the side. At first, I thought the man was joking about the entire thing. The man stuffed the angels into a black plastic bag long before I arrived to pick him up but threw in my trunk. When he began the story, I thought the guy was joker and had a bag of dirty laundry that he was taking to New Jersey.

We had a nice and - believe it or not – normal conversation on the way to New Jersey. Until we passed a Kmart. Then he said "Yo yo yo. You passed the Kmart. We stopped. He grabbed the bag and went took it into the Kmart. When he came back out, he was completely upset. He said they wouldn't even give him a store credit for the angels. The man wasn't kidding about the angels. He believed he had angels in that bag. I dropped him off at his girlfriend's house along with the presumed bag of angels. The girlfriend of the man with the wife and bag of angels appeared to be intelligent and beautiful. It's pure speculation that he, himself, was also a ridesharing driver.

Colleagues

Other drivers - and I've driven enough of them - often provided some of the funnier stories I've heard.

One driver got in and asked how my night was going. The ride was taking him to drop off his own car at a dealership to get his oil changed. I'd taken the driver in the past. He said "Bill, you know I don't let people ride in the front like you do. Last night, a woman jumped in the front seat. First thing she did was rip my phone off the consol. She told me I wasn't getting my phone back until I gave her some dick".

Oh, my goodness. I asked the man what he did. The driver replied, "I gave her some dick". When I asked the driver if the rider was nice looking, he said "Come on now, Bill. That was last night. How can I remember"? We both laughed as I dropped the driver off at the car dealership.

Given the Boot

There was a hotel across the street from that dealership. Several hours later, I had a ping for a ride at that hotel. I picked up a guy and girl and took them from Springfield to Southwest Philadelphia. Nice People. Pleasant conversation. Several minutes later, I realized she left her pair boots in the back seat. I did the responsible thing and called the contact number from the app. A woman answered the phone and said "He did WHAT? I'm gonna kick his ass".

The man would have been a little smarter than to use his wife's Uber app. Somebody got the boot that night, alright.

Highway to Hell

While sitting at a traffic light on Leigh Avenue, I encountered a 9-month pregnant woman. She was standing at an intersection panhandling for quarters. Beautiful girl. Mid to late 20's. I Pulled over and asked her what was going on. She said that she was in an abusive relationship with a man who sold pills for a living in Kensington. She, of course, wasn't on drugs. Oh, no. Not her.

I had a million for her. Then, we relied on a manager of a hotel to put the pregnant woman up. We could find a shelter for her and her pending baby in the morning. Many months later, I was banned by that hotel because they thought I was a "Kingpin for a prostitution ring". That's what their notes indicated in their system when I attempted to put up several other women up in that hotel. That hotel was the only place I could stash these women until a bed was available for them at the local rehabs. Kingpins and pimps make much more than Uber Drivers. I was never a kingpin or a pimp.

While driving the pregnant woman over to the shelter the next day, her phone was blowing up. She was in the lobby using the bathroom and left it in my car. As unethical as it was, I looked at her phone and found the texts to be coming from her husband. The content was pretty much him begging her to get off heroine and come home. He said he worked very hard to be a provider so that they could raise a family. He wasn't a dealer at all, and she wasn't Mrs. Poor Me. She, indeed, was an addict. I learned another lesson of never trusting anybody on these rides. The state ended up taking the baby that I considered adopting. We did not because we realized it would have been a Methadone baby. Not sure how she or the baby are doing. I did see her back on the same corner at the same intersection several months later.

Triplets

Three brothers celebrated their twenty first birthday together at a local bar. I had the fortune to drive them home. One of the brothers wanted to say. The bouncer forced him into my car.

Along the way, he jumped out of a moving car that was going thirty-five miles an hour. His brothers said to leave him there. They said he would eventually find his way home.

Amigos

I had taken three other girls to that same hotel months earlier. All three of them were going to rehab. None of them liked each other. That's how the cards fell while rounding them all up one night. All three of these girls were intelligent.

There were only two double beds but three women. As quick as lightening, they pushed the beds together to form one bed, so nobody felt left out. They took the light fixtures apart faster than an electrician. They didn't want to hit their heads on the fixtures. They delegated tasks to each other to make their stay a little more comfortable. I was smart enough to have the hotel clerks check these women for drugs. That was a prerequisite before providing them with a free bed for the night.

I always asked the hotel staff to make sure nobody entered, and nobody left until I returned in the morning. Anyway, I'm proud that I've been able to avoid too much graphic language with these stories. There was plenty of that in the rides. The names and places have been changed to protect the innocent and the people who aren't so innocent.

Having them sign waivers was a consideration. Amazing how many of them wanted royalties before they would sign. Afterall, it was only their stories, trials, and tribulations. Me? I threw it all together. Other drivers used to tell me they only asked their riders simple questions. They'd say "How was your fabulous Friday?" That's it. They did the trip and kept quiet. Not my style. I asked, instigated, and encouraged.

Pokémon

The games people play. It's 3am. How did you guess? Ride pings for a pickup at Eleventh and Locust. Dead smack in the center of the city. Three University of Penn Graduate – emphasis on Graduate – students get into the car. The destination was somewhere but they kept saying "Make a left", or "make a right, make another left". That was all they said for almost an hour. Guys! Where are we going? Those grad students were chasing Pokémon all over the city at three in the morning. They were completely sober. I thought there goes the future of the country. The Penn Graduate Students are chasing Pokémon all over the city at 3am. Judged those guys too soon: dropped them off at the Schuylkill river at 4am. They were on the Penn Rowing Team. That's a lot more discipline than I had when I was in college. You never know. Never judge a person by the games they play.

Superbowl Memories

The Philadelphia Eagles win. Fly Eagles, fly. I would be flying throughout the city to experience the action on the streets. I could fly anywhere that I wanted throughout the city and get paid for it. As the final gun went off, I picked up a woman and spend most of the trip doubling back to the block I picked her up on. She needed to find her lipstick. Fireworks, cheers, people shouting, and I'm stuck in the rear alley of a home with a rider looking for lipstick. She spent more than forty minutes looking for her darn lipstick.

Good thing the ridesharing company also charges for minutes. That put another couple of worthless dollars on top of a worthless fare. So that's my Superbowl memory.

Philadelphians were well behaved for that Superbowl win. The most notorious event was that a few police horses were stolen from the parade on Broad Street a week later. One of the horses was white and turned up eight days later in...Kensington.

The horse was tied to a parking post at a Wendy's restaurant at Second Street and Lehigh Avenues.

How the heck does somebody steal a white police horse in broad daylight? Then manage to get it all the way up to Kensington without getting caught? Heard the other horse was recovered as well. I loves me some city of Brotherly Love!

Philadelphia's Own

Carefully worded this so I don't get sued. Will Smith is a famous celebrity from Philadelphia. Will has a brother Harry. I've had quite a few celebrities over the years. Use a little surmising and note that I never said Will's brother Harry was one of those rides.

A man gets in from Southwest Philly and is going to the Overbrook section of town. Nice enough man. Puts his pants on just like the rest of us. Normal conversation. He's in the front and drinking a peach soda. The man took an Uber Pool. Two other people join the ride along the way at different times. Before I drop the man off who is drinking the peach soda, another man shouts at us to stop the car. The rider with the peach soda has a brief conversation with the man outside the car. That man leans in the window and asks me if I know who I am driving. He says, "That is Harry Something or other. He is the brother is Will Something or other."

The two riders in the back are in awe. I remain quiet until he gets out at his destination but leaves the peach soda in the console. One of the riders in the back asks to buy the soda for $35. The woman beside him offers even more money. The guy says he wants to "drink the man's DNA". The woman wants a keepsake. An argument ensures between the two over who would get the soda. It becomes a bidding war.

I pick up a rider. She's a regular who has gotten to know me. She sees the struggle with the two in the back. I fill her in on what is going on. She says "Bill, if anybody else tries to take this soda from you, hold my earrings and put my hair in a ponytail". Well after the rides I figured out what that meant. She wanted to fight anybody who tried to take the beverage. The soda ended up in the trash.

Bandmates

Will Smith had a bandmember named Dane Jordan. Make some assumptions. I don't want to get sued. Assume that maybe one day a particular bandmember and his son would need a ride. Assume that they may be going from BJ's Wholesale Club from the Ritz Carlton hotel. Assume that they would buy a lot of grapes and bananas. Enough to completely fill the trunk of a white Toyota Prius. Assume that celebrity wanted to be dropped off at a barbershop in South Philadelphia. Assume his eleven-year-old son needed a haircut. One could probably assume said guys were very nice and would leave their driver a huge tip. But all of that is just assuming. Remember?

Clock Around the Neck

Remember, I don't want to be sued. Anybody remember the celebrity who wore a clock around his neck? Drove him twice. The first time was from a catering hall in Delaware County to Wilmington, Delaware. Fun guy still trying to re-live his youth. Second ride was to a poolside wedding in Norristown, Pennsylvania. Still had the clock around the neck. Still trying to re-live his youth.

Snooping Dog

How about a celebrity who name was Snooping Doggie or something? Got him at an oyster bar in center city Philadelphia. Had a woman with him who I thought was the celebrity. Dark sunglasses. Meticulous makeup. Wow. Knew she was somebody. Asked her for a selfie with her. The snooping dog said no pictures. They I knew they were important. She agreed to the selfie. He said, "just don't tag the location". Fair enough. They were in town shooting a music video. Saw it on YouTube. Good video. Good song. When I dropped them off, he said, "you got the wrong one, dog" and tipped his hat on the way out of the car. Chasing him was pointless. He vanished into the night.

News at Eleven

There were several newscasters. Got a picture with the sexy morning girl that broadcasts out of Market Street. Class, beauty, and fun. Everything she appears to be on the newscasts. The weather woman, however, was more renowned but much less personable. She's been around for years. Many people remember her flaunting her ring on a local newscast. That ended her marriage. The ring was from a boyfriend. Had her cell phone number from years ago. She didn't acknowledge me. I didn't acknowledge her. Her colleague's daughter and I went to Great Adventure together when we were younger. He has since retired. The newscaster's daughter was a total head case. The bathroom lines were long. She opted to use the men's sink while I played the role of lookout. Haven't been to Great Adventure since.

Comedians

Came close to driving a famous comedian from Philadelphia. A crowd was mobbing his limo. I got a ping for a pickup at the same hotel. The ride cancelled as pulled up. It's my belief his "people" ordered the ride as a decoy. I could be wrong. The celebrity was Kevin Hart. Can't get sued for this one because I never said he was a rider. Celebrities rarely tipped anyway. Kevin would have been a good laugh.

Radio Gaga

That would be me. Driving opened some doors. Driving around a radio station manager and his programming director was up there. They never mentioned who they were. I started rambling off some stories to them as I drove. They liked the stories and we clicked. The next thing you know, I am getting an invite to come to the radio station. One led to another then another. There were three big stations in all. One of the better highlights of my driving career. Nothing like seeing the "on air" light come on. Not a word was ever spoken on air about the rides. We talked about anything but the rides. It was a lot of fun. Something I'd like to do again in the future. The door remains open.

Athletes in Town

There were many of them. One of the Philadelphia 76ers was one of my favorites. We took a selfie that was posted on Facebook. A Philadelphia Eagle was a close second. Turns out he lived within blocks of my house. Was traded to Philadelphia by the Cleveland Browns. Young kid. Made me feel so old. Pass his house almost every day. Haven't seen him since. May not be living there anymore or even playing for the Eagles.

Little Sky

That's close to what he calls himself, but it's been altered. Picked him up just outside the city. He was going to Millersville University. Maybe he was a student. Maybe he was performing. He didn't strike me as anybody famous. Probably because he was so young. He walked the walk and talked the talk, though.

The guy was wearing a nice shirt. It called for a compliment. "It's a Supreme", he replied. I had no clue what a Supreme was. The shirt, he said, cost about fourteen hundred dollars. He then offered "I have eleven bands in my back pocket". I thought the guy meant that he was a promotor of bands not realizing band meant a thousand dollars. The guy had money. Two years later, I see him all over the news. The guy blossomed into one of the more popular rap artists. Pleasure to have driven an up and coming star.

Swedish Overload

Bright sunny day in the city of Philadelphia. I rolled up to the curb. Seven Swedish Foreign Exchange students waiting for their ride. They had requested a large passenger van and weren't smiling when saw a white Prius pull up.

There was no way seven beautiful women and one handsome driver were going to be able to fit in this Prius. They were in a hurry to get to their destination. I was in a hurry to stuff all those beautiful women into the car. They agree to get in. I agree to take them. We were smiling. I was smiling.

Wasn't easy fitting them all of them into the car. There was no way I was going to let this ride go. Stuffed them in like sardines. Three were in the back. Three were up front. One was spread out between the front and back. They were singing and rubbing my head the entire time. We pulled up at their destination. It was the Liberty Bell.

The security guard screamed at me to stop the car. He said it is illegal to have that many people in the car. I screamed back at the girls get out! The ride was over anyway. I needed some selfies first. We had to illegally park to squeeze in a few more selfies. Kind of like when we squeezed the girls into the car in the first place. How many more of those rides was I going to be able to take? Plenty of them. PLENTY of them!

Moonlight Feels Right

We'll see the sun come up on Sunday morning. And watch it fade the moon away. I guess you know I'm giving you a warning. Cause me and moon are itching to play. Rutgers's cheerleaders! The wind blew some luck in my direction. I caught it in my hands today.

They were coming from an after-hour's bar. It's time to play. Can still hear them singing into my ear "Your eyes are as big as the moon" blah blah blah. Of course, they were as big as the moon! They were cheerleaders, drunk, and singing into my ear. Whose eyes wouldn't be as big as the moon? I offered to take them on a trip beside the ocean. And drop the top at Chesapeake Bay. Ain't nothing like a sky to dose a potion. The moon'll send you on your way. The cheerleaders got out of the car instead.

The High Way

Life is a highway. I wanna ride it all night long. If you're going my way, I want to drive it all night long.

I always drove sober. Other drivers didn't. I get a ping for a ride. There's this guy running down the highway when I go to pick him up. He's all kinds of out of breath. No buildings, no houses, or anything else in sight.

When I picked him up, I asked where he was coming from. He said he jumped out of another rideshare. The riders and the driver were indulging in a cloudy, illegal mess of smoke. The rider couldn't take it, so he jumped out and ordered another ride. Can't say that I blamed him. I would have waited on a corner rather than run down the highway. Guess that was because he was a little frazzled. Wasn't like they were going to grab him and drag him back into the car. Then again, maybe they would have. Riders and drivers are strange people.

Asia

That was the name of one rider and where she belonged. This country has no room for people who don't know how to smile. Miserable woman.

Shoeless Joe

I'm driving down Market Street in Philadelphia after dropping off a rider. I look in the rear mirror. Darn, if that guy running down the street with no shoes on doesn't look like exactly like my last rider. The Mummer's Parade ended the day before but there's always a straggler or two floating around. Thought it may have been a Mummer with a hangover or still drunk. Homeless people sometimes don't own shoes, but they don't usually hang around in that vicinity. Then I see the guy's hands waiving in the air like Old Gory. It was my rider.

Not sure what happened to his shoes, but his suitcase is still in the trunk. No wonder he was running down the road. His train to New York wouldn't have been the same without his belongings.

Shoeless man. Shame on you.

Mushroom Country

Another carful of riders. They're never as pleasing to the eye when they're all males but often have been the funniest rides I've taken. These guys were West Chester graduates. They should have known better to want a ride at 2:30am to Kennett Square. Considering they had no other reason to go there at that time of the morning other than to get a cheesesteak.

I wasn't thrilled to take that ride. There was no way I'd get a ride from Kennett Square that would take me anywhere close to home. There are a ton of steak shops much closer to where we were. Good ones, too. Tried my hardest to talk them into any other place. South Philly would have even been a better ride. Wasn't happening. They were fun guys, though.

Drunks laughing and making fun of each other is always entertaining. The sad part was that by the time we got all the way out to Kennett Square, there was nothing open. Not even sure if Kennett Square even has a cheesesteak place. Plenty of antique shops. No steak shops.

Their sole reason for picking Kennett Square was because it is the mushroom capital of the world. They were in the mood for a mushroom cheesesteak and thus assumed they would get the best one in Kennett Square. I offered to take the poor guys back at no cost, but they declined.

Their heart was set on getting mushrooms one way of another. Morning wasn't too far away and the bench I left them at looked big enough to hold five guys. This driver is ALL about a good cheese steak but, Kennett Square? Here's a useless piece of information you may already know: Mushrooms only grow in the dark.

Defining Freelance

It's not rare to pick up an attractive, yet intelligent woman who is riding by herself to a sporting event. It is rare that they aren't meeting up with a friend or relative. This was a first for me. We talked the entire ride. Very friendly.

At some point in the conversation, I asked the woman what she did for a living. She was brief in saying that she did Free Lance. You would think a writer would want to talk a little more about her profession. I respected her privacy and didn't press her with questions. I mustered up the courage to ask this woman why she was going to a basketball game by herself. Threw that question out there in one quick breath of hot air fearing it was a violation of her privacy.

She responded that she had never been to a game. She turned thirty-two years old and that it was time. So, we talked about music. We talked about current events. By the time we got off at the stadium exit, there was a wall of traffic. I hadn't seen line of traffic at a Sixers game in a long time. We waited and waited. Extra time means extra money. It's way better to keep rolling than to watch seconds tick off the clock from an earnings per-spective. Ridesharing pays better on distance.

Extra time is calculated in pennies on the hour. At this point, I suggested she may want to end the trip and walk the quarter mile or so to the entrance of the stadium. The Free Lance writer wasn't happy but agreed. I suggested she walk around the twelve-foot iron gates. She said "Are you kidding? I'm going right over those gates". I laughed. While sitting in traffic, horns started blaring and people were cheering the woman on. The woman pole-vaulted over the gates faster than you could say freelance. The sight was spectacular!

Several months later, three guys were going to a strip joint in another section of the city. After dropping them off, a woman screams my name and comes running across the parking lot. "Bill! It's Kelly". Kelly who? She doesn't look like any Kelly that I know. Not dressed in that stripper attire. I don't know any Kelly like that. She must be talking to somebody else. "Bill! Remember me? You took me to the basketball game back in October. It's Kelly", she screams. Holy...So that is what the definition of freelance meant. She was a pole dancer. A stripper. Explains how the woman scaled that fence so easily that night. Really expected Kelly to ask for a ride home or somewhere that night. She didn't.

Good thing that she didn't because there was another couple coming out of that strip that joint at the same time. I had driven that couple a few months prior. Had no idea the two of them would be at a strip joint. You never know with people. There had been a lot of times I'd driven couples to a strip joint. They waived hello and kept walking.

It's a shame the "freelance writer" wasn't taking tips from people waiting traffic that night at the game. Bet she would have raked in a small fortune. Wouldn't have had to split it with the strip club, either.

A Hostage Situation

Society Hill never impressed this driver. Houses there go for two million dollars and have one bathroom. Not all of them, but enough of them. The people are snobby, rarely tip, and the conversation is always one sided. Stereotyping is wrong. Consider this a generalization. There's a difference. Pick up was down one of the smallest streets in the world. Rider didn't come out on time. What a surprise! Got out and pushed the buzzer to the gated community. Nothing. Several minutes later, the gate opens. I drive in thinking the snobby rider expected total door service.

The gate closes. The rider cancels. Trapped. Trapped because the security guard wasn't going to let me in and had called for a tow truck. Pleading with him did no good. The guard didn't want to hear anything. Thank God another woman saw the ordeal and made a call who her boyfriend who threatened the guard. The gates went up. The rat escaped. Scary.

These Boots Were Meant for Walking

Took the same woman on three quick rides. Usually the ride-sharing company wouldn't allow that to happen. Algorithm or something that prevents it from happening. Not sure how I was able to pick up a woman on Chestnut Street at around 11pm and take her one block away. Her feet hurt. She parked a block away but wanted a ride to the club. I go around the block.

Ride pings again for the same woman. She wanted a ride back because she got the wrong shoes. Didn't want to pay for a ride back to the club because she was cheap. Ping. Got her a few minutes later. She was carded and not getting in the club and still had sore feet. Surges hit Center City hard late at night. She paid a pretty penny to go to the club, back to the car, and back to the car again. Can't remember the exact cost for the three rides but it was in the double digits. Somebody should invest in a better fake ID. Maybe allocate enough money in her budget for multiple rides when carded. The woman either didn't know how to smile or didn't want to flash that smile in the direction of this driver. Oh, somebody was smiling afterwards. It wasn't her.

Headed Towards the Danger Zone

Friends and family had been advising me to stay away from Kensington. Easier said than done. Many riders were going there because of the gentrification taking place in Philadelphia. They weren't gentrifying fast enough. I developed relationships with a lot of addicts that required closure. "Make sure this person gets the help" kind of relationships. The place was like the wild west.

Kensington is the most notorious drug areas in the country. Kensington Ave is the foundation. The el runs above the avenue, run down stores clutter the avenue, and people live on the avenue. In tents, in abandon buildings, and on sidewalks. It is an accepted way of live. The place has a distinct smell driving down the street.

People have said the city of Philadelphia allows certain activities to exist. It's easier to monitor than it is to eliminate. One section really stands out.

Paradise City

Take me down to the paradise city where the grass is green, and the girls are pretty. It wasn't paradise city. It was Emerald City. It's on Emerald Street off Lehigh Avenue. Some of the most intelligent and artistic people you will ever meet live in Emerald City. Many of them come from good homes. Many of them ended up living in cardboard boxes in Emerald City because they couldn't deal with life's stresses. Some of them ended up there because they had other challenges. Some had mental issues. Just about all had dependency issues. Often, I've asked which came first: Did the drugs cause the mental issues or did the mental issues cause the drugs. Doesn't matter.

Have Yourself A Merry Little Christmas

Already finished up with the family thing. Wanted some extra cash. Did the ridesharing. As usual, the first ride was taking a guy home from Glenolden back to Kensington. It's 9:30 at night. Christmas night. I see a girl I recognized as one of the women who lived under Emerald Bridge. She is crying. Her hands are wrapped in two bath towels and soaked in blood. I pull over. She tells me a "date" took her up the hill and tried to rob her of her last ten dollars. She wouldn't let go of it. Enter a boxcutter and ten of her fingers. You've been spared a lot of graphic details. You're welcome.

The woman had spent most of her years on a lobster boat off the east coast. There were many times I tried to help her. One time, I managed to talk her into going to Temple hospital because she had an abscess on her hand. That, I learned, often came from an addict missing the vein while attempting to shoot up. While in the hospital, others wanted to get in for the same reason. One Saturday night, the car was full of addicts willing to go to the same hospital.

It was a scene directly out of One flew over the coocoo's nest. one of the girls was trying to steal food off the food card and another fell asleep on the elevator. People were stepping over the woman. Other girls were trying to steal cringes from medical carts. I was chasing them all over the hospital trying to maintain order.

When all were collared, everybody was in the woman's room. The woman was bartering some of the few clothing she owned with the other girls for drugs. They all had ways to hide their drugs. Little did I realize the other girls even had drugs on them to barter. That was the second to last time I ever saw the woman. Have yourself a merry little Christmas. Let your heart be light. From now on your troubles will be out of sight.

Helping Hands

The woman needed help but refused a ride to the hospital. Had she not gone, she would have bled to death. It was my turn to solicit one of the addicts to help get her into the hospital. What a role reversal! They were usually trying to solicit me for cash to buy drugs. The closest addict lived on the corner less than a few blocks away from the incident. Her name was Annie.

Many times, I'd offered her help Annie. She was a girl I had gotten close with during her many attempts to get into rehab. I trusted this woman to help get the bleeding woman to the hospital.

Annie was a likeable person. Her "friends" used to say "Bill, don't help her. She is screwed up even when she is not screwed up". That was a line I would never forget, and it was true. Annie was also a very kind woman. Five kids, a husband, a boyfriend and more "clients" than you could imagine. Many of the girls on the Ave referred to her as "Sporty" because of the way she dressed. On this night, Annie was going to become a set of helping hands to help a set of hands that needed help. I pick her up, we force the bleeding woman into the car and get her into the hospital.

Close but No Cigar

It was time to drop Annie off at her house. We'd gotten the bleeding woman into the hospital. As soon as we pulled up in front of Annie's house, many cop cars came out of nowhere.

One of the cops shouted, "What's her name?" I replied "She is sitting right here. Ask her yourself". Not a good move. The police were implying I'd picked her up as a "date". The incident was explained to the police. They tell me they've been watching me for quite some time. I reply "If that's the case, you know what I do. I get them into rehabs, shelters, or to their parole officers".

The police agree do a little research and come back over. The lieutenant and I have nice talk. We exchange information. She says to be careful in the future.

The Bleeding Hands

The woman who required all the stitches to her hand never stayed at the hospital. She found it much more important to get back out on the streets for her drugs than to take care of her health. Later that night after she left the hospital, I rounded her up again and took her to a few other hospitals. None of them wanted her.

The hospitals said she had no insurance. They said take her somewhere else because she was an addict. On the last attempt, I started taking pictures of a woman who also had several broken ribs because of the attack. The front desk nurses saw me taking pictures and called the guards.

The guards wanted my phone and the pictures on the phone. After being detained for a bit, I left with the pictures, with the girl, and with the phone. The Too little, too late. The last we spoke, she had seven open heart surgeries. Not good. I liked the woman. Her name was Heather.

Planet Fitness

While getting out of Dodge, a ride request gets cancelled right before the rider gets in. It was near the bus depot. Another woman sees the Uber sign and does what others have done and jumps in the car. She's told it doesn't work that way. The woman pleas for me to take her across the busy intersection. It was impossible for her to walk across that stretch of highway. Roadwork and construction.

Fair enough. We ride. The woman drops her phone between the seat and the console. It rolls to the back seat. She's sitting in the front. She tries to lean into the back seat to retrieve the phone. What a beautiful site! When we get to the gym, she asks me to wait one second. She comes out crying and asks to take her to one of the most expensive high rises in the city.

She has decided to clean some units rather than work out. It's a cold Sunday night. Nobody wants their units cleaned without notice on late on a Sunday night. Turns out the woman – with a cell phone, nice clothes, and in great shape – was homeless. The bag of clothes she was going to take to the laundry mat were everything she owned. After sitting with her while she did the laundry, I ended up putting her up in a hotel for the night. We are still friends. It was a family issue at the time.

The woman was a graphic designer with a degree. She was employed by one of the biggest clothing designers in the country. Thank God she was able to resolve the family problem and maintain her life. That after having slept in the Planet Fitness for the last thirteen days. That's why she was crying. They wouldn't let her stay anymore. Anybody's life can change for better or worse in a blink of an eye. Never take anything for granted. It's that old saying "There go I by the grace of God". Be glad you're breathing. When you're down, know you're alive! Things are never as bad as they appear. Ask the lady from Planet Fitness!

The Planet Fitness woman had strong family ties to Atlanta. She wasn't the only one. Another normal, intelligent rider grabbed a ride from Springfield. The rider was in her early thirties and as normal and presentable as they come.

Driver's Seat

Doing alright. A little jiving on a Saturday night. Jenny was sweet. She always smiled for the people she'd meet. On trouble and strife. She had another way of looking at life.

The ride was a roundtrip to Germantown. Germantown still has some nice sections. Great conversation all the way there. We get to the destination. It wasn't a pharmacy as indicated. It was a "Poppy Store", one of those Mom and Pop shops that sell every-thing from cereal to drug paraphernalia. Jenny said she would be right out and headed back to Springfield. She said, "Kill the lights and park up". The phrase "Kill the lights and park up" was one I'd heard too many times in Kensington. I sensed there was trouble brewing.

Jenny was quick. Upon returning, I asked her if she needed help in any way. "What do you mean" she asked. Trying not to offend the woman, I mentioned there were a lot of other riders that I've helped along the way. that have had addiction problems, etc. I was careful not to insinuate she was a person with issues.

Great Expectations

Jenny quickly changed the conversation. One of the better ones I'd had in quite some time. Told her I couldn't help noticing how well she spoke. She offered up that she had gone to an upscale finishing school in Atlanta. Much like the character from Shake-speare's Great Expectations.

Do Not Enter

When we arrived back at her house, Jenny told me she appreci-ated the ride and great conversation. She offered me to come in. Wasn't happening. After politely declining by throwing out that I had a family to get home to, she said she only wanted to talk. There was something I mentioned along the way that she wanted to discuss further. I knew she meant the "challenging issues" that had been brought up as we arrived at the Poppy Store.

As pressed as I was for time, I told her I'd make all the time in the world to talk about a struggling issue she may have. We could sit out front of her nice home or grab a quick bite to eat and discuss. Jenny appeared upset at that moment. I felt bad for being short with her and asked her to tell me what was going on. We sat out front of her house for a considerable time. The story she told me was amazing. I agreed to go into the woman's house to further the conversation. I told her that going into a rider's home was nothing I'd ever done in the past. I pleaded with her not to put me in a dangerous situation. She agreed. It was never her intention to harm me.

Enter Anyway

The house was nice. It was clean, furnished, and had a very homey feel to the place. There were elephants everywhere. They were hanging from the ceiling, all over the sofa, painted on the walls – everywhere! So, I see you like elephants, huh? What's that all about? "My ex knew I liked elephants. He bought me a few". Alrighty, then. Nothing that could be stolen from me was taken into her home. Not my iPad, no cash, nothing. The cell phone was glued to my hand with 911 pre-dialed and ready to go in case needed. We just talked and talked and talked. Jenny insisted I first take my shoes off. I ask guests to do the same thing. We laughed and I complied. She made herself comfortable and suggested I do the same. My coat never even came off. Hers did. And some other clothing. Wait a minute! I'm outta here!

The nervousness could be heard in my voice. Not the kind of nervousness one would think. The woman clearly had no intentions to seduce me nor did I have any intentions of seducing her. She had no intentions other than to talk and made that clear again. If being in comfortable attire was easier for her to talk, so be it.

Before the conversation continued, I moved to the front door and told her I was still listening. I'd just rather stay by the door just in case. This was the first time a rider was willing to pay for an ear. The only reason I stayed near the front door rather than escape was because of that story she started to tell. We entered her home.

The house was a one-bedroom loft. There was a sitting room, a bed, a bathroom, and an area to eat. Younger people living in the city are into this living. Often younger people don't have or want a refrigerator. Most of their time is spent outside of their abodes. The woman moved about the room lighting a million candles and offered me something to drink. I believe she poured herself a glass of wine and that made me nervous again. She moved into the bathroom and brushed her teeth. The door was more than ajar. She told me she would be out in a minute but wanted to change into a pair of sweats. Elephant Sweats. Her underwear had elephants on them, too. Just saying.

I needed to hear the rest of that story and get out of Dodge as quickly as possible. (While proof reading this story, my wife said "No, you need to get out of there, screw the story!"). The woman sat on the edge of her bed after pulling a chair over for me to sit on. No way. No how. She said we could talk out back, but it was going to be cold out there. This man totally hates the cold. She wanted to tell me a story that she claimed she had never told anybody. I was all ears. Out back we went.

Trouble Ahead

The woman's mother may have had a drinking problem. They were traveling down a desolate road out in Amish Country in the wee hours of the morning. Just the woman and her mother. A head-on collision ensues, and the woman's mother perishes instantly. There's nobody else on the road and back in that day, nobody had cell phones. The long walk was roughly four miles. She had no other siblings. Her father struggled to raise his daughter. At the breakfast table almost a year later, the man takes his own life in front of the girl. The only other family she has is an aunt who puts her on a bus to a boarding school in Atlanta.

The frightened girl gets off that bus while stopped at a rest stop and runs away. Shortly after, she has a change in mind and gets another ticket to continue the trip onto Atlanta. I believe she said she was almost sixteen at the time.

While waiting on the next bus trip to Atlanta, the girl believes she lost the ticket and can't afford another one. An older "gentleman" offers the frightened young girl another ticket. It wasn't free.

He befriends the girl. They travel throughout the state of Florida for several years. He does everything with the girl that would warrant a life in prison. Significant damage is done to her body and – worse – to the girl's mind. A body can heal. A mind takes much longer. We all go thru life with some sort of scars which affect our daily lives.

Yellow Brick Road

When are you gonna come down? When are you going to land? She's not a present for his friends to open. This girl's too young to be singing the blues.

While being held captive and "shared" with other criminals, the girl manages to escape. Jenny is one of few who reports the perpetrators, gets thru counseling, and rights her ship. Completing school was one thing. Completing finishing school was another. This girl was a lady. A damaged lady for life.

Nobody wants to admit they can use therapy. Not even me. We can all use good therapy. The problem is that they're going to tell us to eat right, exercise, and get a good night's sleep. For that reason, I, myself always believed I could work through things without one. I'm smarter than any councilor, right? They will spend hours, days, weeks, and years milking that cow until your insurance or cash run out. That's just my opinion. What we really need – each of us – is somebody willing to listen to us. Learned that from many of the addicts I'd encounter in Kensington.

People used to say they wanted money, drugs, whatever. My experience, for the most part, was that they really wanted a good ear. Of course, they wanted the money and drugs, too. Just weren't getting that from me. Those "challenged" people often were excellent therapy for me, too.

They also served as an escape from many other things like the recent passing of my father. The stresses of the full-time job. A taxed marriage over living with sickly parents. Mix in a crazy rescue dog and the potion was complete.

When Jenny said she had never told anybody her story, that's for her to know if it was the truth or not. I interpreted her "not telling" were some content that I will not mention here. We connected instantly. Some of the issues she struggled with that I can talk about her struggles with men. Remember, this woman had a lot of horrifying things happen to her by more men than you can count during her ordeal.

I initially told her I couldn't come in, I had family at home, etc., I don't believe any of that registered or she didn't believe me. Brushing her teeth and changing with the door ajar was testing me. Jenny may say otherwise. I know. Maybe I was testing myself. Who knows? Most normal men would have struggled with the temptation. I can be honest enough to say it wasn't easy. Jenny wasn't my first cup of temptation. Thank God, nothing happened with her or anybody else that you are reading about. Mistakes have been made. Plenty of them. Taking advantage of these people or crossing lines was not one of those mistakes.

Bad Boys. Whatcha Gonna Do

Whatcha gonna do when they come for you? I backed out of my driveway. There was a police officer sitting at the bottom of my street with his lights out. They do that all the time. The previous night, I passed a different officer on the street over and asked him how the fishing was going. He replied "not good tonight. They must be able to see me". We laughed and he drove to a better hiding spot.

This officer pulled me over seven houses after I pulled out of the driveway. "Why did you stop me officer"?

"Where did you get the car, Bill? Your lights are out".

"It's a rental car. Nice try. The lights come on automatically".

Pulled a rough draft of this book out of the sun visor and handed it to the officer. Told him I was dedicating an entire chapter to the heroes in blue. He flipped thru it and said, "drop a copy off at the station when you get a chance, Bill". Well, here's your chapter, officer.

Boys in Blue

We'd bump into each other all the time at local Wawa's. That seemed to be the final stop after Ubering. Nice pint of iced tea that I wasn't supposed to be drinking, a few Tastykakes, and a laugh with the cops. The running joke was who was going to get the most drunks off the streets? Me or them. A little competition is always a healthy thing.

County cops have a different reputation than city cops. In the county, people think they have nothing to do so they gang tackle everybody. In the city, they think the cops just don't care. Only once have I had a rough incident with an officer. He cited me for talking on my phone while driving. Beat that citation. Not guilty as charged. Phone records proved that.

I can say that the cops have helped me out more than I can ever write about. They are people just like you and I but brave enough to do what they do every day. I trusted them enough to bring the struggling addicts to them. None of them were ever arrested. They never let me down.

Straight Jacket

One woman told me she had tried rehabs so many times but always left them shortly after entering. She said the only way she was going to be clean was if somebody 302'd her. I'd done that a few times. Legally, they were always sprung a few hours later. They needed a cop do 302 them.

Picked her up in Kensington. Told her I had a few cops that could help 302 her without charging her. At first, she wasn't having any parts of that. There was nothing I could do or was willing to do unless she was willing to dance the correct way. Knew she probably had drugs on her. Wasn't getting in the car with them.

I called the police and told her she wanted help. They advised me to bring her to the Wawa so she wouldn't feel so intimidated as if she would feel going to a police station. I videotaped the woman saying she was going to the police to be 302'd. That was in case we were stopped along the way before we got to the police at the Wawa. All went well. They got her into a hospital and filed zero charges of possession against the woman. Of course, they confiscated her stash – but no charges were filed.

Incidents like this were the norm. Girls like her, were the exception. She was one of two women I'd encountered that had full blown AIDS. There was no way of telling by looking at the beauty. Sad thing was that she was still out on the streets selling herself to support her habit. People say that happens. Probably much more than one thinks. The police knew what was going on. They always said the same thing: "If you're going to try to help them, just be careful. It's not as simple and easy as you think". Better advice was never given. Thank you, officers.

Serial Mom

Some of the paying riders were more dangerous than the addicts on the street. In the Parkside section of town, there was a nice woman who appeared young enough to pass for sixteen. She was a mom in her mid-thirties with a voice and body of a teenager. We laughed and talked the entire way. It was the second to last ride of the night. She said she was on her way over to her husband's girl-friend's house to kill her. It went right over my head because she kept talking and laughing. She changed subjects like crazy. Sweet woman.

The following morning, there was a huge butcher knife in the back seat. The blade was more than a foot long. I'm no expert but it could have even been a machete. Took a few pictures of it. Notified the ridesharing company. Couldn't be sure it was hers. Doubt if it was the ride after hers. In any event, somebody's husband's girlfriend wasn't killed by that knife on that day. She may have been killed but it wasn't with that knife. That knife ended up in a dumpster far away from the woman's house. I remember watching the news and scouring through the internet. Nobody was stabbed or killed in Philadelphia that night. Try doing a search on that in the city of Philadelphia. On second thought, maybe you may want to save yourself the time.

Ambulance Driver

We weren't just ridesharing drivers. We were ambulance drivers without certifications. Countless times, rides pinged for people going to hospitals with an emergency. The first time, a young guy has me pick him up in West Philadelphia. I tell him I have no medical skills. He responds by saying "it's okay. You guys are faster and cheaper than an ambulance ride". He was suffering from carbon monoxide poisoning. His bosses truck apparently had a faulty exhaust system. Along the way, the man insisted I stop at a vending truck. They were selling sneakers at a low price. It was the first of four stops for sneakers down Broad Street. We eventually reached Temple Hospital. A sale is a sale even if your life depends on it.

Ambulance Driver II

Another woman was a frequent flyer to the hospital. Can't tell you how many times I picked her up at her apartment and took her to the emergency room. She lived roughly eight blocks from the hospital. It was always the same thing. She was having heart palpitations and it was always on a Monday. Go figure. They weren't bad enough to prevent the woman from screaming at the same guy on the phone. This happened every single time we drove to the hospital. The language she used. Wow!

Low Rider

Take a little trip, take a little trip, take a little trip and see. Low rider knows every street, yeah. Low rider is the one to meet, yeah.

Picked a guy up who wanted to impress the three women he was with. He thought riding in the trunk would do the trick. The women didn't find a thing funny about the guy wanting to ride in the trunk. I was on a mission to find every single pothole in the city that night. Wanted to teach the man a lesson. Rumor has it there are over 250 million dollars' worth of potholes in and around the city. I believe I had found every one of them during my time driving for the ridesharing company. His ride wasn't long enough to experience all the potholes, but I made sure he got his money's worth.

Before you go assuming I was cruel for doing that to the rider, maybe I should note that he wasn't drunk. Just the kind of person who had a lot to say to and about a driver who was just out to earn a supplemental living. His words got him in trouble that night. The good news was that he said he was studying to become a chiropractor. He now can use his own back to experiment on.

I admit there were times I wished the ridesharing company would charge riders by the pound.

Good Fellas

It may also have been wrong to leave a few Swarthmore students in the city of Chester in the middle of the night. They were such good fellows. Chester isn't exactly known as one of the safer cities in Pennsylvania. Swarthmore is usually considered safe. That night, those guys were going from a bar in Swarthmore back to their dorms. They were hungry. I was hungry, too: for a tip. So, I offered those guys a stop along the way for food. They said there wasn't any place still open in Swarthmore at that time of the night. The closest place would have been Chester. Some chicken wings. It was slow that night and late. Figured there would be no more rides. Stopped the clock and drove them to Chester for their wings. They said "please don't leave us here. We will only be a second". They were more than a second and it pinged for another ride. Sorry boys.

I can still see the expression on their face. They came out and there was no car waiting for them in that section of the city. Maybe they should have been a little nicer to the driver.

Simple Simon II

The Swarthmore students reminded me of some riders from a long time prior. I picked up a group of guys going home from a bar in Media. They were so drunk and obnoxious. The nicest of the four was named Simon. Told you there were four Simons. His friends wanted him dropped off at the top of the street. They all – including Simon – lived at the bottom of the street. His friends said every single time they go home, Simon pees in the middle of the street. They didn't want to be seen with him this time even though it was the middle of the night. Simon was funny. His friends were annoying. Simon wanted to go to the casinos. His friends did not.

I follow their request and drop Simon off at the top of the street. He could barely walk because he was so intoxicated. The other guys get dropped off at the bottom of the street. Almost instantly, I get another ping for a rider on the same street. It's Simon. In that short period of about two minutes, I didn't even recognize him. I tell him I dropped off a few drunks a minute ago. They lived on his street and that one of them wanted me to take him down to the casino. Simon replies "It's me. It's Simon. I'm going to the casino".

He was a fun ride. He left his wallet back on his street. Probably while he was relieving himself. We had to go all the way back and then back to the casino again. I had Simon on many occasions after that night. He was very intelligent. Many of the drunks usually are. Simon's managed a chicken joint. Anytime I get the chance, I go through his drive through window and ask him if he's ready to go to the casino. He always is ready. Manage that chicken, Simon. Catch you on another night.

Money

Money. Get back. I'm alright, Jack. Keep your hands off my stack.

Drunks were usually generous. In hindsight I wish I had accepted their tips more times than I did. One guy came out of a strip joint with a wad of cash in his hand. He wanted me to drop his buddy off a few blocks away. Threw a twenty on the dashboard. Wanted the heat turned down. Threw another twenty on the dash. The radio changed. Another twenty. This went on for the entire ride. Can't tell you how much cash was thrown all over the car that night. Scooped it all up and stuffed it back into the man's pockets. I didn't want him sobering up the next day and being without all that cash.

You know what's funny? Most people who tipped seemed to be people who were struggling financially themselves. There are people who used to say that's the reason they were struggling in the first place. People who can't manage their money aren't bad people. Nothing goes with us when we die. I'm hoping the generous people who tipped well get front row seats in the afterlife. People who relied on tips as a part of their earnings rarely tipped themselves. Strange but true. You always knew what to expect from the riders who would say "best rider ever. Will leave you a nice tip on the app". Nothing! That's what we expected. People who advertised that they were going to tip were always the ones who never left anything.

Manoa Road

This brings me to rides in the city vs rides in the suburbs. People always said stay out of the city. It's dangerous. Let me tell you a little something: The suburbs had most of the crazy riders. Driving in the city was easy. The roads were flat, the rides were short. The destinations were right there. In the burbs, you would get the craziest of crazy. Nobody knew where they were going, and we spent the better part of the night dodging deer and fox. In the city, the only thing there was to dodge were potholes.

The suburbs were a place where a rider got in and had a stolen road sign with him. It said Manoa Road. Somehow, he managed to tuck the sign between the seats without me seeing it and then left it in the car. No worries. The next rider was a police officer who thought I was the one who stole the sign. Sorry, officer. I'm just the Uber getaway driver. The cop and I argued over who was going to keep the sign. He wanted to return it to the borough. Wasn't happening since he was unable to produce his badge. He was a cop. Just an off duty drunken cop. Guess who still has the sign?

The best of the best were the rides who went from the city to the suburbs then back to the city. Surprising how many ridesharing people had to see parole officers in the suburbs. Yet, still lived in the city. Those rides paid well because they were so long, and I would often get to pick them up again and take them back to the city.

Momma Mia

I had and still have a full-time job. I provided payroll services, marketing strategies, and card processing for local businesses. Most interaction is with the business owners. I'd often speak with a several clerks at various places. One such clerk was a local girl named Mia. She was fresh out of high school with flaming red hair. Loved her cocky attitude. She was quick with a remark here and there. Mia worked at a local pizza shop. I'd gone to school with her parents, her uncles, and knew many of her family members and friends.

Born to Run

The highway's jammed with broken heroes on a last chance power drive. Everybody's out on the run tonight but there's no place left to hide.

After dropping off a rider at Clearfield and Kensington Avenues, I explosion ensued. A staggering woman fell to the ground. I put the car in park, steadied her into the car and heard another explosion. A second girl falls to the ground. Then a third explosion. Another guy is helped into the car.

So now we have two girls in the back seat. Both are young. Both are pretty. A man is in the front seat. I'm focusing on getting out of dodge and trying to avoid gunshots. Thinking I'm going to die in Kensington, I pull out my iPad and video the entire episode.

The guy is on speaker phone with his mother. He is screaming at his mother to get him the heck out of Kensington. After all, it is her fault he's chosen to live a life on drugs in Philadelphia, right? The girls are comforting each other in the back seat. One of the girls is dope sick. The other is as well but just not as bad.

As I'm on the phone with the guy's mother, one of the girls pulls out a needle and is trying to get the other girl well. At that time, I'm screaming to the girls "no drugs in this car" while at the same time, trying to keep the guy's mother on the phone. The scene was chaotic.

I look back again and recognize the tall redhead. She is from Delaware County and worked in a pizza shop. OMG! "What the heck are you doing in Kensington"? The look on her face was that of shock. She was embarrassed to have been recognized. I need to talk to this girl. Alone.

The others get dropped off to safety. The redhead and I have a conversation. To this day, she insists they weren't firecrackers instead of gunshots. I insist they were. Experts who've seen the video on Facebook agree. They were gunshots. None of the three were hit. That's all that really matters. It was close to a holiday. Maybe the Fourth of July. Maybe Memorial Day. That gives credibility to her theory that they were fireworks.

Oh, baby this town rips the bones from your back. It's a death trap, it's a suicide rap. You gotta get out while you're young. Cause tramps like you, baby you were born to run.

It's A Small World

It's a world of laughter. A world of tears. It's a world of hopes. And a world of fears. It's a small world after all.

I throw the video on Facebook. It gets over nine hundred views within several hours. Nobody recognizes Mia in the video. All is fine with the world.

Mia was living in an abando in Kensington. I'd reached out to her on numerous occasions. On one such occasion, she is with a "friend" and taking pictures on my iPad. I want her to get help. She wants the pictures she took but has no phone. We barter. I will post them to Facebook if she goes into rehab. We agree. She only has a limited time to find a phone and download the pictures. No way was I keeping pictures like that on Facebook.

It's the middle of the afternoon. Not many people were on Facebook. None of my friends would know the girl. I was wrong. A councilman sees the post and asks if its Mia. Another guy says "that's my niece. And on and on it went. I couldn't delete them fast enough. Many people had assumed Mia was dead. They hadn't seen her in years. Finally, somebody posts "that's my daughter". WOW!

Now it became a different game. I wanted her home to her family more than any other person I encountered in Kensington. Eighteen separate times I'd try to get her home or to rehab. One day she was ready to go home. The sight of her in her mother's arms was worth every minute spent in Kensington.

It was short lived. A person will never get help until they are ready. There isn't a thing a person can say or do to help them. Within a few hours, Mia was back in Kensington. It set the foundation in her head for hope. That was important. She had it all. Eventually it would happen if she could survive in the meantime.

You Say You Want A Revelation?

Well, you know. We all want to change the world. You say It's evolution. Well, you know. We all want to change the world.

I was attempting to take Mia to rehab for the umpteenth time. One of her "friends" – also an addict - wanted to tag along for the ride. Mia wanted to stop at a laundry mat before going into rehab because she had no clean underwear. She hated me telling her that she didn't need underwear in her profession. I was implying she was a prostitute. She didn't take kindly to that. Her comments are too unsuitable to print. That was the way she spoke. She was tough on the outside but soft in the middle. Mia liked ice cream. She was usually willing to talk over an ice cream cone.

As I was sitting in the car waiting for the Mia's clothes to dry, her friend asked if she could tell me something. She claimed she never told anybody. You know my ears were totally open.

She alleged that she had been in Kensington for a good number of years. That was the place she chose to go because it was the drug capital of the world. This woman claimed to be one of nine women abducted in Cleveland years ago and held in a basement for years. It made world news. Couldn't tell how old this woman was but I'd have thought she would have been older if she were one of those women. Hard to tell some of their ages down there. The guess is usually on the high side because most of them had tough paper routes and hadn't aged gracefully.

This woman claimed to be in her late thirties. Maybe that coincides with the woman's age from Cleveland but who knows? As she started telling the story, Mia gets back into the car. Normally, she wouldn't pay attention to this or any other story anybody was telling. This story was way too hard not to pay attention to.

The woman not only claimed to be one of the women but claimed to be "The" woman. The woman who managed to escape from that basement in Cleveland and get help for the rest of the woman. If her story was indeed true, it was one of – but not the most – fascinating stories I had heard. There must be a way to research the truth.

The woman claimed she was living a normal life in Cleveland with a husband and two small girls. On her way to work one day, she stopped at a post office to drop off some mail for her employer. That's when she was abducted by the monster. After being chained in a basement for years, she escaped. I just wish I remembered how long she was held captive, but it was long enough where she had been presumed dead.

Her parents had passed away and her husband exercised his right to a divorce. He remarried a woman and moved to Alabama. Her kids were grown. Her husband suggested that it would be too disruptive to have the woman re-enter her children's lives. Hard as it is to believe, that's the woman's story and she was sticking to it. Mia is sitting in the back and looked at me thru the rear-view mirror. Her eyes were bulging. Not the first time they were bulging while in my car but this time they were BULGING! The story we were hearing was unbelievable.

Mia never made it into rehab that day. Gotta give her credit for yet another attempt, though. Not sure what happened to the other woman. All I know is that I took her somewhere later that day to talk to a counselor. They allegedly were going to have her on a train to Alabama within a few days. For all I know, the woman may have been trying to muster a little cash out of the dumb driver out of sympathy. That wasn't happening. People come and go in Kensington. This was one woman I never saw again. Just hoping what she said was true and that she got on a train to Alabama.

Seasons in The Sun

We had joy. We had fun. We had seasons in the sun. But the hills that we climbed were just seasons out of time.

Mia and I had many encounters. I liked her and knew she was too young to throw her live away in Kensington. I'd go the extra mile to do anything I could to get her out of there. She wanted it. I wanted it. Getting there was the hard part. She was never quite ready.

The time that hurt the most was while taking a few other girls into rehab. We see Mia on Kensington Ave. I, again, offer to take her in with the others. She agrees. Before she gets in, I insist that she doesn't use in the car. She wants to make a deal. If I let her, she would go in. Deal.

I allow her to do it. It's a sickening feeling to let somebody do that. Almost immediately, she starts to get out of the car. Wasn't happening. I was in a rage. I open the trunk and take her belongings and throw them up and down Kensington Avenue. I'm shouting all kinds of obscenities. Everyone from the addicts in the car to strangers on the street were staring. It was wrong to treat her or anyone else that way. She was struggling. I couldn't watch her self-destruct. To this day, I haven't gotten over my behavior. Mia was never welcome in my car again.

Hello Again Stranger

One night after dropping off the previous rider, I bumped into Mia again. It was in the middle of the night. The last several hours were spent getting some addicts into rehab. While driving one of them to a crisis center, I heard a woman scream "Bill, its me". No way was that girl getting into my car under any circumstances. "I just want to give you a hug. I earned my own money. I have my own drugs. I just want a hug". It was the highlight of the night. The hug was sincere. It was good to know Mia was still alive. Not where I had hoped she would be, but alive. She still wasn't allowed in the car.

Friends with Benefits

Technically, we weren't friends. The benefit was to come. I'd seen Mia several times since the night we hugged on Kensington Avenue. This night was a cold night in January. Mia had no place to stay. I was trying to help another woman who had challenges other than drugs. I'd met the woman on Kensington Ave. Surprise. Surprise. The woman's name was Penny.

Penny was very athletic and attractive. She came from a good background and was educated. At one point, she was a competitive gymnast and a personal trainer. It's my belief that Penny's parents may have been strict or had too high of expectations on the girl.

Her problems began after breaking her femur bone. The pain pills didn't last forever. Then came another form of making the pain disappear. Then another. Penny's habit wasn't as bad as others. She explained that challenges in her life were making her do drugs. That's often the case. She wanted help via proper medications or therapy but didn't know where to turn to. We explored several places. Nothing was available on a Friday night at that time and it was getting cold.

There was that hotel who'd done me a few favors and put people up for the night with no charge. I didn't know the girl well enough to trust her there alone. Annie, who'd helped me in the past, was my first call. Annie said "Bill, there is no way I am leaving my warm house to stay in a hotel with a stranger. Call Mia".

That's where the benefit came in. It would be a benefit to me with Mia standing guard for the night. It would be a benefit to Mia to be able to get out of the cold for the night. I trusted Mia. It was a done deal and Mia was allowed back in my car for a ride or two. Friends giving benefits. She had a place to stay for the night. I had a watchdog for my newfound friend, Penny.

Who Let the Dog Out?

Who? Who? Mia and Penny wouldn't get out of bed in the morning. I tried everything. Neither of them was budging. We were up against the clock. Penny needed to be at the crisis center early in the morning. Checkout was nearing and I needed woman would get out of bed. Time to roundup a watchdog. I texted Annie. She said to come pick her up. After doing so, we headed back to the hotel. Nobody messed with Annie. The girls were given marching orders and hustled out of that hotel. Annie also made sure they made the beds and cleaned up their trash along the way.

The ride back with the three women was awkward. None of them liked each other. They were telling negative tales about each other. I never knew who to believe. Things worked out in the end. Each girl was taken to a different location. Ride over.

Penny Hardway

Penny and I had a few encounters. The altered last name isn't far off from her real name. It is alarmingly like the famous basketball player. Hardway is appropriate because that's always how she did things: The hard way. I mentioned Penny earlier. She was the athlete who had her share of challenges. Like many, I liked that girl. The last time I saw Penny was back in September. The weather was getting cold. She was still trying various rehabs. I'd taken her to several and kind of gave up on her.

One night, Penny asked for help a final time. She claimed she was ready. I told her I wasn't messing around. It was straight to rehab. She wasn't getting picked up in Kensington and wasn't allowed to have anything in the car. For clarification, I told her I was calling her mom. She agreed.

Penny's mom was a nurse at an area hospital. When I picked her up, I told her that Penny was going straight to the hospital. No stops. I did the best I could given the female anatomy to make sure she had no drugs on her. We drove straight to Chester. She had taken something before getting in the car. Her words were slow. Her actions were slow. She was comprehensive.

When we arrived at the hospital, Penny almost seemed to be asleep. I went into the lobby and grabbed a guard for assistance. By the time the guard and I got to the car, Penny hit herself in the neck with a needle. She slumped and fell outside the car door. Other medics came rushing to help. She was blue and not moving.

While the medics focused on Penny, the guard focused on me. There were a million questions. I didn't know the condition of Penny and assumed she didn't make it. The guard said I was going to be charged as an accessory to murder for allowing her to have drug paraphilia in the car. What a complete joke! It was, however, enough to put me in full panic mode. I'd called my wife and was home by three in the morning. My first call was going to be to my lawyer. The second call was going to be to the hospital to have the guard fired. It wasn't my first pony ride with that guard. His focus was always more on me than on the addicts. The man had issues.

I'd posted a picture of Penny on Facebook saying goodbye. She was one of the few I'd friended along the way. The attempts were that plentiful to get her into rehab. Soon after the post, I had to alter it. Penny – still alive – saw the post and messaged me. The message said "I'm sorry. They hit me with Narcan. I'm alive and in Kirkbride Rehab". That was the biggest relieve. Often, I'd had my share of scares. This one hit way too close. Penny is another amazing person with her life ahead of her. The rehab attempt didn't go well. I'd heard from her several times since then, but it's been a while. My prayers go out to her in hopes that she is doing well.

Defender

A rider who had an addiction problem long before I met her turned her life around. She was an interesting rider who was now going to law school. I friended her on Facebook just to watch her progress. Often, she would comment on a hater's remark about addicts. She once commented to a hater that one day she would be prosecuting him. That made me smile. The woman is going to stick it out and becomes a lawyer. I can feel it. Many people relapse. Hoping she's not one of them.

Minor Mistake

Literally. The girl was a minor and a big mistake was made. Not by me. The guy who ordered a ride for the sixteen-year-old girl was twenty-eight years old. It was two o'clock in the morning. The man did his share of partying with the girl then called for a ride to get her home.

The girl started to get sick on the way. Nobody, luckily, ever got sick in my car. I wasn't going to let her be the first. As soon as she started to heave, I threw it into park, ran around the car, and scooped the girl up and out. She did get sick. Only on herself, though.

When we arrived at her house, she insisted she didn't live there. I didn't know what to do with this minor. I called the guy who set the ride up. He said, "leave her there". Not happening. I drove the girl back to the guy's house just as his wife was arriving home. I scooped the girl up, placed her on their lawn, and told his wife to deal with the situation. Other people may have called the police. I wanted to but was talked out of it. It wasn't my responsibility, it would have only hurt the girl, etc.

So, I hit the man in the pocket. Two Hundred dollar clean up since the girl got sick in my car. Wink wink. To this day, I still wish I had called the police instead.

10 Pounds of Maryjane

One of the earlier riders was also one of my favorites. Our first of many rides came from Chester. It was the street of an old girl-friend. We went to college together. This rider lived a few doors down from her. His ride took him from his home back to a half-way house in Philadelphia.

The rider and I were opposites completely. He was of Muslim faith, younger, and had been arrested for possession of marijuana.

Having struggled with all those addicts, I certainly wasn't a fan of a man who was selling narcotics. The ride went well. The conversation went better. He told me what led him to being arrested.

The man was more than a recreational user. Ten pounds of marijuana is a lot of pot. His story was that he had been selling and buying. One night, a police officer stopped the man. With a lot of marijuana! The officer was ready to let the man go with only a citation. He only wanted the man to be honest. "How did you get here" the officer asked. "I walked", the man replied.

The problem with that is the officer asked him to lean against a car for a pat down. The car belonged to the rider. The rider's keys pressed against his pocket. The car alarm went off. "You walked, huh" said the officer. Game over. The man ended up serving three years for possession with intent to distribute.

The rider and I became friendly. He had his share of issues, but I liked the guy. He made me laugh. He was always sincere. He offered cash if I were willing to become his personal driver to and from the halfway house. Not sure how many rides we took together but it was a lot. The man was a guy I will not forget. Hope he is on the right track to a better life.

Useless Fact

More crashes are caused by people texting and driving than drinking and driving. Please keep that in mind before you get behind the wheel. It would be nice for this to be a lifesaver instead of a useless fact.

Chiropractic Driving

Many hours behind a steering wheel can cause a little back pain over time. I had a rider accelerate the process. She had a long trip from the city to Valley Forge. She wanted to smoke a cigarette. I wouldn't let her. The woman kicked the back of my seat for over forty minutes. Thankfully all that driving over the years didn't require a trip to see a chiropractor. The woman didn't hurt either, but she did report me for not letting her smoke. Unbelievable.

Ride on The Wild Side

Holly came from Miami F.L.A. Hitch-hiked her way across the U.S.A. Plucked her eyebrows on the way. Shaved her legs and then he was a she. She said, hey babe, take me on a ride on the wild side. Said, hey honey, take a ride on the wild side.

Two o'clock in the morning. A cold Tuesday. One of those rare weeknights I pulled an overnighter. Nothing was going on with the full-time job the following day and I couldn't sleep. Ride pings for a pickup on Interstate 95 South. I go north and south several times. No rider. When I called her, she said she was at the Renascence Hotel right off the highway. Not a problem. Told her I would be right there. "She" gets in. She is about 6'4 with an Adam's apple and wearing a dress. And heels. Ok. Whatever. I start the trip. It says drop off on Interstate 95. I need a more specific destination. She says "Just drive. You and I are going to have a lot of fun". At that moment, I was ready to jump out of a car going 55 mph. I can still see her bulging eyes staring at me thru the rear mirror. I gave her another chance to provide a destination. She again repeated "I told you to just drive".

Instead of jumping out onto the highway, I reacted quickly. I said "Great. You're into that stuff. I am, too. Let me get a condom out of the trunk". She fell for it. I opened the rear door, grabbed her by the neck, and threw her onto the highway. I was thinking, "hey babe, take a walk on the wild side". I sped away. The police were called. The ridesharing company was notified. No Combat pay that night. Things weren't always easy. It wasn't the first transvestite. It certainly was the most memorable. Others always minded their own business and were often fun conversation.

Turn to Paige

Here I am. On the road again. There I am. On the road again. There

I am. Up on the stage. Here I go. Playin' the star again. There I go. Turn to Paige.

Her name isn't really Paige. This man is too cheap to pay her royalties so, Paige it is. Paige had two problems. The first was that I was happily married. The second was that she was thirty years too young. In event that my wife ever puts me on Curbside alert, I intend to only date five years north or south of my age. Paige was a baby. Let's just leave the young girls to friends who are having a mid-life crisis. My friend, John, may be having a mid-life crisis. He's driving a Corvette. He's not in the market for a little eye candy, either though.

They weren't really Paige's problems. She was a third-generation addict. Smarter and attractive than a lot of others. I met Paige when she was walking down Kensington Avenue. I'd wrapped up another episode with a struggling addict when Paige offered to help. She presented herself well. When asked why she was in that area, Paige replied that she could only afford an apartment in that rundown area. She was a medical biller.

We walked down to her apartment because it was getting dark. Paige told me she had a record because the cops had grabbed her in the same area while coming home from work. The prostitution charges stuck, and she was on parole. Hard to believe but I gave her the benefit of the doubt.

Paige and I grew close over many months. She had a lot of insight to the neighborhood and would often tell me who to help and who not to. I trusted her. On several occasions, addicts would not have gone into rehabilitation without her help. Eventually, she confessed and told me she as well, was a recovering addict. It was hard to believe! No trust was lost. After her hearing on the prostitution charges, Paige served a little time. She was mandated into a recovery house. I found her a job. She continued to help others and life was great.

Paige called me one Monday night and said she had taken a Xanax. That's against house rules. It was the night before her mom was to be sentenced for drug possession and robbery. Her father and brother were also users and their lives were taken by drugs. I beelined to her recovery house and arrived at the same time as her parole officer. He'd known me from other addicts and trusted that I would get her help. "Bill, you have four hours to get her back into a rehab or she's going to jail.

Wasn't easy to do because she only had Xanax in her system. We must have tried eleven different rehabs to no avail. The parole officer was willing to have her stay at our house until we were able to get her in somewhere. It was the first and only time an addict was taken to our house to stay for a few days. My wife wasn't happy in the least. This isn't the final chapter with Paige. There's more to come.

Tailor Made

The haters in the world often asked why I was willing to help female addicts and not male addicts. Truth is, there were several men. They didn't grow like trees out in the open. The women walked the avenue because it was a source of revenue to support their habits. Men often lurked in alleys and robbed people or places to support their habits. Tailor is an incorrect spelling of the last name of a male addict I helped get into rehab. He was one of the kindest people I encountered and said he had no family support.

Paige and I made a few attempts to get the struggling man into rehab. He had nothing at the time. It's nice to be able to say that he is now doing well. There's nothing better than that occasional phone call from him. He has his own apartment, is working as a carpenter, and recently purchased a car. The kind man also has regained the trust with his family. This is one guy I never want to lose touch with.

Free Samples

One ride in the badlands was with a father of two small children who were going to school. It would have been cheaper if he walked them out to the car and relied on this driver to get them to school. Some parents wouldn't trust the driver. This guy didn't trust the neighborhood. He was correct with that assumption.

As we were going down one of the streets on the way to the school, a mob scene was running down the same street. As we got closer, we heard somebody yelling "samples". That made this driver want to park the car and see what kind of freebies were being handed out. In Kensington, they were drug samples. I must have been the only one not knowing that.

It was quite the sad scene. There were professional people, teenagers, and everywhere in between diving for those samples. Dealers often offered the samples so addicts would patronize their products. Sad. On this occasion, the dealers threw empty plastic bags into the air. People scrambled all over the street to retrieve the empty bags thinking they were full. That's an image etched in a mind. Sad. Very sad.

Express-O, Please

Many riders would figure out a lot of ways to beat a ride-sharing program. It previously was working for the company, the riders, and the drivers. Roughly in the middle of 2018, the company came out with a product called "Express Pools". Some riders thought that meant express as in fast. No stops. No picking up other riders, etc.

What it really meant was that the drivers didn't have to go a specific address to pick the rider up. They would meet the driver at an intersection, instead. The purpose was to make it quicker and easier for the drivers. Cheaper for the riders. Riders would manipulate the product by ordering an Express Pool. They would call the driver and insist he or she picked up at their house. It was too cold. It was raining. Whatever reason they could come up with. They were getting door to door service for the lower price.

If the driver didn't comply with the request, the rider would make sure to let him know. They would trash our ratings after the ride. They had us by the throat. We complied.

On one such occasion, an elderly gentleman ordered an Express Pool. He was going from his retirement home to an Acme on the mainline. The rider opted to take the front seat. We pick up another woman on her way to work. She is running late.

The time comes for the elderly rider to get out. He says he was supposed to go to the supermarket and not the intersection where he was getting dropped off. It's pouring rain and very cold. He couldn't have been a day under eighty. I felt bad for the guy and was willing to take him the remaining distance to the Acme.

Before I could offer, the woman in the back shouted "Bitch, you ordered an Uber Express! Get your ass out of this car and walk". It was quite humorous. She was in her early twenties. Funny because I no longer had to take the man a little further. Not funny because he was older, and it was raining so hard. She was completely out of line in yelling at the man regardless of his age. We came to a happy medium by dropping the woman off first and then taking the man back to the supermarket. He tipped. It was a win for everybody. I can still hear that woman shouting those obscenities from time to time.

Those Express Pools were a huge reason to eventually walk away from the ridesharing. They were more aggravation and less money.

Hey Baby

On this Express Pool, forcing the rider out was my decision. There were two such times I made a rider get out. It was early in the morning. His friend ordered him the ride. Not that I cared, but the man was gay. Every word out of his mouth was baby: "Baby, it's cold in here". "Baby change the radio station". "Baby what time is it"? That went on forever. The man was impossible to deal with and very demanding.

The second rider gets in and she is a sweetheart. The man says "I don't want her in this car, baby. Make her get out". Then he says "you're dropping me off first, baby. I don't care what the app says". That went on forever, too. By this point, the poor girl in the front has had it with his comments. I politely ask him to show a little respect for the woman. The man calls the guy who ordered the ride for him and says things that are too crude to print. The car stops. I open the door. I politely assist the man out of the car. He is kicking and screaming the entire time. Sorry, baby.

Rude man. Somewhere there's is a guy complaining about a nice driver who had enough of his nonsense. Rides like this were starting to become the norm as opposed to the exception. The clock was ticking. Thoughts of stepping back were becoming more frequent. First, there was more money to make and more fun rides ahead.

The Greener Mile

This rider looked and sounded like an actor from The Green Mile. The big guy. Not sure of his name. We were driving down the expressway late at night. Thank God there weren't a lot of cars on the expressway. He was drinking a bottle of water and passed out. The bottle remained in his mouth for most of the ride. There was a fear that he would drown. I took the chance he wouldn't because he was no fun before he passed out.

At some point on the expressway, he woke up and said he had to pee. The next exit was a considerable distance and there were probably no places open, anyway. The man was going to have to wait. He repeats it in a loud, threatening voice. "I gotta pee". There was no waiting. His wish was my command because of his intimidating size. I stop the car in the middle of the expressway. The man relieves himself, and cars dodge the staggering man. Not a pretty site. The man is alive. He was or also alive when I dropped him off. Beyond that, I couldn't tell you if he is still alive. At some point, That is going to hurt himself or somebody else with his drinking ways. It just didn't happen on this ride.

In Through the Out Door

In a better part of the city early in the morning, a blue-collar man leaves his house for a ride to work. We don't go far, and he is pleasant enough. He's dropped off. It pings for a different. The rider is going to that same address where the previous man lived. I thought it was the same rider, so we picked up where we left off with the conversation. Maybe the guy had to check into his office but worked from home. Maybe he forgot something.

It was a different man. Puzzled, but I never asked him where was going. He voluntarily offered he was on his way to bring his mistress over a little breakfast. There was no way that I was going to volunteer that I took his mistress's husband to work on the previous ride. Most people like a little variety in life. Not this woman. The man could have passed as the first guy's identical twin.

To this day, I wonder if it was the first man really going back home. The only reason I doubt that theory was because of the second man's anxiety. He couldn't get into that house fast enough. Strange things happen in South Philadelphia. Strange things!

Paige

Remember Paige? She'd been doing well staying with my wife and I while we tried to get her into rehab. She was attending her meetings faithfully every night. We would spend most of the mornings trying different facilities. Each one would tell her "There's nothing in your system. We can't admit you".

Keystone in Chester said to her "you're an addict. You know what you need to do to get in".

And she did. Without my wife or I knowing she hid her drugs inside of herself. Around seven o'clock at night, Paige went up to shower before going to her meeting. A lot of time passed. "Give her some privacy" my wife said. Mr. Patience went upstairs anyway. The water was running. Paige wouldn't answer. As I prepared to go out another window and onto the roof, my wife forced the door open. In a puddle of blood and a needle laying on the ground, was Paige.

OMG. OMG. They were the only words that I could manage. We called 911. The paramedics and police arrived quickly. Narcan is a drug that is administered when an addict experiences an overdose. Two hits of Narcan were used. Just as you saw on the movie Pulp Fiction, Paige springs back to life as if nothing had ever happened.

Somehow, she managed to sneak some heroine past us and used it to have something in her system. In doing so, she would be able to get admitted into rehab. It didn't work.

The ambulance took her to a local hospital. All her vital signs were normal. They released her. There was no moving her to an impatient program. No beds were available. They did not take her to jail. No charges were filed. What to do with Paige?

Hi honey. We're home

My wife would freak out if Paige were taken back to our house. There were no other options at that time of night. I slept on the floor beside Paige for the remainder of the night, fearing she would again use. It wasn't a good night.

Early the next morning, we headed to a crisis center in Chester. Paige wanted no parts of that. She threatened me to no end. She was going to call all my clients in the processing business and tell them I supported addicts. She was going to notify my friends that I was hanging out with prostitutes. Anything you can imagine, Paige was going to make a claim.

The only thing that mattered was getting her into the crisis center. There was nothing to hide. Obviously, my family, friends, and many clients already knew what I was doing. I forced Paige into the crisis center. It was a process that would take several more days and she continued to stay at our house. Every few hours, I would have to tell my wife it would only be another few more hours. She wasn't happy. Paige ended up getting into Keystone Recovery a few days later.

One of the responding officers saw me at a Wawa later in the month. It was embarrassing. I felt the need to explain who the girl was and why she was staying at our house. The officer was understanding and kind. His sister was also a heroine addict. It's a disease. It's a choice. Everybody has their opinion in that ongoing debate. What really matters is that they are somebody's daughter, somebody's sister, etc.

Family and friends suffer more than the addicts. The addicts are usually comforted by whatever substance they are using. Their families are the ones who deal with the worries and concerns. Sad.

Much has been brought to light about the opioid crisis in recent years. I knew little to nothing about it before driving for the ride-sharing program. It's real. It's getting better. It has a long way to go. Amazing how little is done. Heck, a driver can tell you every corner where things are sold. Why can't the police figure it out and shut them down? It's not as easy as it sounds. That's something I always asked myself. That could be a book within itself. It was nearly impossible to include these stories because they happened all the time. Always while driving in the middle of the night. Again, sad.

Shhhhh

Your secret is safe with me, sir. You're not the only one I drive to the bar at 6am. Just after that ride, the next rider gets in and announces he is a mental patient. "Don't worry, I won't hurt you, though" the mental patient said. He clearly fit the bill but was a gentle and kind man. Most of the conversation was him expressing his views on the mental health system. It sounded like he needed a drink. Maybe I should have dropped him off with the other rider that was going to the bar at 6am.

Fire and A Walk

I'd taken a rider home to his house around eight at night. The man lived so close to my house and that made it the last ride of the night. When we pulled up, the house was ablaze. Few walls were standing. It was impossible to get down his street.

One can only imagine how the man felt nearing the neighborhood. If it wasn't his home, certainly it was a neighbor. I felt the same way, having lived so close. You could smell it before you could hear it. There was a mob scene on the block. The man's dog perished in the fire. I will never forget the man begging somebody – anybody – to take his dog for one last walk with the man.

A hero complied and scoped the dog up. The man and the hero walked a block while the firefighters continued to extinguish the blaze. It's a story I've tried to forget. It is a story I will never forget.

Saint Emo's Fire

It's four in the morning. A scrapyard fire started in the badlands around ten the previous night. Smoke from the fire could be seen from Pennsylvania, New Jersey, and Delaware. There's an underpass known as Emerald City where homeless people live and do drugs. The scrapyard is within a block of Emerald City. It's one of the most notorious drug sections Philadelphia.

Fire personnel evacuated all the residents within several miles. Not the addicts. They are walking up and down the street and conducting business as usual. Some of them were getting a free shower from the water running over the top of the bridge. First shower in a while for many of them. The police and fire personal are focusing on keeping everybody else away. They continue to and extinguish the fire. There is soot all over cars and homes. Many residents needed a shovel to remove the thick soot from their sidewalks.

Marching drums are blaring. They had a terrific beat. Emo is marching towards the fire with two adult drummers dancing alongside of him. There is a trail of kids behind Emo and the drummers. Entertainment at it's finest while the city is ablaze. While writing this, my wife walks into the room. She says, "there's nothing funny or entertaining about this story". I beg to differ. She may have missed the point. Those folks in that area may struggle but they sure know how to entertain themselves. I highly recommend you watch the video. It's posted all over the internet as well as on my Facebook account. Hysterical. Honestly. Hysterical.

Norwood To Morton

Stole this story from another driver. She isn't getting royalties. Her rider was picked up in Norwood and was going to her house in Morton. When they arrive, the rider was totally intoxicated and said, "this isn't my house". The driver asks her where her house is, and the drunken rider says "just drive. It's down the street".

This went on and on. Seven times. Each time they would go around the block, the rider would say "it's wasn't her house'. That wouldn't happen if I were the driver. We'd have figured something out upon arrival the first time. There was money to be made on other rides.

This driver was content driving around and around with a drunk rider in her car. After all, we were compensated on time and distance. I had many rides like this ride. The only difference was that this driver continued to drive around the block.

Other drivers often shared stories with me. Some of the stories were from their riders. Many of the stories from their riders originated in my car. I was the driver of the rider who told them the story. Many drivers didn't believe the story they told me happened in my Prius. Small world.

Miss You

Hello there. The angel from my nightmare. Paige is out of rehab. I pick her up and am taking her to her brother's house in Bensalem. It has been twenty-nine days of therapy, detoxing, and counseling. She looks good. She feels good. Paige wants to stop in Kensington. Not happening. Couldn't believe she wanted to go use again after being clean and sober for close to a month. Blew my mind. Coincidentally, her mom calls her on the trip. From jail. Her mom encourages me to let her make a stop. My ears weren't hearing things correctly. Again, I'm threatened just like she threatened me when she went into rehab.

Annie Get Your Gun

I needed another addict's help again. Who better to turn to than Annie? The girl who, people said, Annie and I originally met a year prior. She asked why I never offered to help her. Because you're the girl who's "screwed up even when she's not screwed up". I asked if she was serious about getting into rehab. She replies "Can you take me to the pharmacy? A client sent me money via Western Union". She didn't want rehab. She didn't want money. She wanted to cash out on some money she had already earned. She really was screwed up. But she wasn't "screwed" up at the time. Not sure why, but I took Annie to the pharmacy.

She was a likeable person. Had half a million kids. Smiled a lot. Seemed to be honest. Hid nothing, including her addiction. She usually only wanted to talk. That seemed to be the case with most addicts. I contemplated re-naming her Weirdo so I wouldn't have to pay her royalties. Weirdo was something Annie always called me and probably everybody else.

I turned to Annie to help with Paige. They both knew each other. Neither of them liked the other. While Paige was threatening me to take her back to Kensington, I messaged Annie and told her I needed help. "What's up, Weirdo", Annie replied. I messaged her back telling her about the problem. Annie messages me to bring Paige to Kensington. She wants me to swing by and pick her up first. When we arrived in Kensington, Annie jumps into the back seat. She shouts to Paige "What's your problem"? Paige replies "I don't have no problem". Annie shouts back "then get out of this man's car". Problem solved. Long story short, Paige is doing well and has been clean for over a year. She has a job, a nice boyfriend, and just bought herself a car. So glad that things are working out for Paige. She has her entire life ahead of her.

Annie is still struggling. We message a lot. I'd really like to see her complete her program and get the help she needs. She's always asking for a ride to probation, a ride to the clinic, a ride to the pet store. You know Annie is a good person. She puts that cat over herself. She'd rather go hungry than have that cat miss a meal. Hopefully, good things will happen for her in the future. I worry about her.

A Black Kia

This car was home to a middle-aged couple. They kept it parked underneath Interstate 95. Both, one could tell, were refined adults at some point in their lives. The woman had the smile. The man had the sincerity. They dressed like they lived. They were in a community of others with the same issues.

Their "supermarket" was Emerald City. That's where they would get their drugs. They opted to live in their car because they were fortunate enough to own a vehicle. Most other addicts slept under a bridge. This couple panhandled for a living. They were at the foot of the exit ramp to the highway on most days.

I'd see them often. They wanted help but were never ready. I'd do as much for them as possible. Most times, it was dropping her off at the corner of her "supermarket" because they didn't have enough gas for the car. Sometimes, it would be a ride to a place with a bathroom. Can't tell you how highly I thought of this couple. They were different than the rest. They were also very nice people. It was sad. They will later be called Kate and Jerry.

Cross Country on a Bike

A younger Asian guy was one of the longer trips. Took him from Broomall to JFK airport in New York. The first thing that struck me was that the rider had nothing. Not even a toothbrush. He was going to China for few weeks. The kid was too lazy to carry anything with him on the trip.

He was all but lazy. He was wealthy. The kid claimed everything he would need on his trip back to China was there in China. He did have a skateboard. That was the only thing he brought with him.

The conversation was great. His language was challenging. What impressed me about that kid and the ride was the kid's perception of America. He was a foreign exchange student attend high school in the states. It was a good high school. A private high school.

When the kid first arrived, he had the perception that America was dangerous. He shaved every hair on his body to make himself appear younger. Then he boarded a plane from Philadelphia to Chicago the second day after he arrived in the states. From Chicago, he rented a bike and rode it all the way to California. The kid was maybe sixteen. It was always something he wanted to do.

The ride took him months. That's how he spent his first summer in the United States. Takes a lot of courage to do what he did. He shaved all his hair believing thugs would not rob a young kid while he rode a bike across country. He was never robbed. Had nothing to do with shaving any hair. That kid is going places one day. Its going to be further than Chicago, California, or China. The kid had willpower.

Dry Clothing and an Ear

Erica was an older woman. By older, I mean forty-two. Younger than I but older than most addicts in Kensington. I liked Erica.

She was married and the mother of two. Her oldest was eighteen. Her youngest was nine. We'd made a lot of attempts to get her into rehab. She was also one who was asked to leave the hospital in Chester because that guard believed I forced her there. Erica stood up for me and told the guard off. I appreciated that from her.

She could never get over the hump. Her husband had enough and refused to let her back into their house until she was clean. This isn't the time to trash him, but women aren't supposed to have to be paid by their husbands for sex. He was that low. He was a bully and a chauvinist. All of Erica's problems couldn't be blamed on him, nevertheless.

The last time I spoke to Erica, she was sleeping on the sidewalk on Kensington Avenue. I'd recommended that she go to Prevention Point because there was a code blue alert. They didn't have enough beds, so she slept on the sidewalk out front that night. There was a cold freezing rain most of the night. Erica called me and asked if she could borrow some dry clothing until the morning.

It's the worst feeling in the world to tell somebody you can't do that. She wasn't asking for money. I didn't sleep a wink that night. The following morning, I got to Kensington before the sun came up. She wasn't there. I knew a few other places she used to go. She was asleep under a frozen piece of cardboard. Some hot chocolate and she was on her way to Fifth and Spring Garden. She was ready and had hit an all time low. I'd keep my promise to her. If she went in, I'd stand by her throughout recovery.

Erica went into rehab. I kept my promise and went up to visit her. Things were going well. She was calling frequently with updates. That was until a woman who was just released from Kirkbride reached out to me. She said, "I heard you are Erica's man". What the heck was she talking about? The addict claimed Erica told her we had been sleeping together before she went into rehab.

That couldn't have been further from the truth. I never crossed any lines with her and had nothing in common with this woman. I liked her and respected her and understood her struggles. Period. After that call, I never reached out to Erica again and blocked the number to the rehab center. She may still be in recovery. I worry that she may have fled. There was a person or two that I wanted to help. They would never be given that chance.

Much like the ridesharing, the Kensington days had to end as well. I hope Erica successfully made it through rehab.

Beth

Beth, I hear you calling. But I can't drive you home right now. Me and the boys are playing, and I just can't turn around.

Beth is going to have to find her own way into rehab. It made me sad. I liked Beth and wanted to help her turn her life around. I saw so much potential in the woman but had to stop trying to save the world. Another beautiful woman who would have to find her own way. Oh, Beth what can I do? Beth what can I do? Had a sixteen-year-old son. Every day I hope Beth is doing alright.

Seminary Mistake

He's been all over the news lately. He was another priest charged with sexual assault on teenagers. Can't be true. We met at a previous job, I had hired him. It was his first job since coming to the states from another country. Promoted him to management. Worked with him for seven years. Nicest guy in the world.

The man had gone to our wedding. We stayed close for years. We lost touch. He went to Seminary School and later became a priest. The priest called me towards the end of my shift. He needed a ride to the airport. The ride was at 4am. He would pay me well. I was willing to cut him a break on the fare. It was more of a favor and had nothing to do with the company I was driving for.

He paid me nothing when we got to the airport. Didn't offer a penny. For over a week, I thought that was out of character for such a fine man and priest.

Now he's been all over the news. Arrested the other day. Now I understand why he was going back to his home country and offered nothing for the fare. Everybody has problems. I hope the accusations are not true. He was one of my last rides.

Stuttering Mike

Don't be a hater. He gave himself the nickname. The app only listed the rider as Mike. This guy was a lot of fun. I drove him a few times. He was a little slow and always trying to beat the system. He owned a body shop in South Philadelphia that wasn't doing well. Stuttering Mike said it would be the last time I got to drive him.

That's because he decided to trash his own body shop and make it look like a robbery. He was out on bail pending a court date. Mike may not have known there are cameras everywhere in South Philadelphia. He smashed a few of his own windows and scattered gray paint all over the walls of his shop. Mike lived across from this shop and carried the empty paint cans to his own trash can out back of his house. His footprints led from his shop to his house. Not the brightest guy in the world. Maybe he will get off on parole. Everybody else does. His laugh will be missed.

Black Kia No Mo

This one's a happy ending and it means a lot to me. The couple who were living out of the black Kia were finally ready to go to rehab. They'd called his father who was living in Australia. The man had money. He was willing to put them up in a hotel in Center City for the night until I was able to drive them to rehab in the morning.

Jerry and Kate had enough of living in their car. Before going to the hotel, their car hit one of the many potholes in the city. It broke the car's axle. There was a garage across the street. Jerry's father was willing to pay the seven hundred for the repair. The shop said they would get tow the car in for repairs. Jerry, Kate, and I went out for a bite to eat.

The police towed the car before the mechanics had a chance to tow the car. That was the final chapter for the struggling couple. They would spend a night in a nice hotel and go into rehabs out of state. They suffered a lot prior to that. In my opinion, there wasn't a nicer couple in the world. Jerry is in a rehab in New Jersey. Kate has completed a rehab in Delaware. It makes me sad that they are no longer together. She is in a new relationship and recently bought herself a new car. Kate is pregnant with the child she always wanted. She can raise the child without assistance from the state because she is also working now. Words can't express how happy I am for all of them – especially Kate! I will always be there for her. Kate deserved more. She's on her way to having a better life. She is going to be a great mother and wife. Good luck, my friend. We will meet again down the road.

Settlement to Rest in Peace

I met Nicole in Kensington while helping another. Action news snapped a picture of me scooping a girl off the street. The girl was staggering down the road. I'd just dropped off a man to a vigil for somebody who had been shot and killed. There was a large crowd and the news was covering it.

I saw this woman and asked the police to help her. They told me not to worry about it and said, "it happens all the time". That's when I scooped her up. Nicole approached me and asked if I needed help with the girl. She looked like she had issues of her own but insisted she was clean. "Then why are you walking like that", I asked her. She said she used to be an addict. She was struck by a car and spent almost two years in the hospital. Plates, rods, and pins were inserted all over her body. She lost every tooth in her head.

I asked why she didn't pursue the driver who ran her over. "I'm an addict. Nobody would ever believe me". I took the girl to my attorney's office. It was going to be a tough case. The lawyer took the case and sixteen months later called me and said to bring her in to his office. He had a check on his desk for her. It was a large amount of money.

I was thrilled. Some money was coming back to me for lending the Nicole enough money to survive until the case settled. She had been clean for over a year and a half. It couldn't have had a better ending. Nicole and her kids would have enough money to get out of Kensington and have a good life.

I rang Nicole's phone off the hook. No answer. Nicole was robbed that morning of her Suboxone and got sick. Word has it she went to Emerald City and a five-dollar bag brought her down. Nicole passed away. You can't make this stuff up. The lawyer posted on my Facebook that I had done the bulk work and he was going to set up a trust fund for the kids.

Nicole's viewing was very sad. There were few people there – mostly arguing family members. All of them were decent people living in a rough neighborhood. I tip my hat to Nicole's father. He really tried his best to provide for his daughter. My heart breaks for Nicole's sister, Kelly. I'd gotten to know Kelly over time. She, too, is a good person. Some days I just can't figure out how life works. That's my struggle. Every single day.

My Way

I started to tire of doing the ridesharing. The company cut our earnings on trips. It was New Year's Eve. Biggest money night of the year. At least, it used to be before they hired a million other drivers and dropped the rates considerably. This year, I didn't even want to play the game. It was raining. It was cold. I just didn't want to do it. But I went out anyway.

The first pick up on New Year's was two attractive young girls. I got a ping for the following ride before those girls got out. That rider called to make sure I was coming. The girls were on speaker phone laughing with the guy. He asked them not to get out until he was picked up. They agreed.

The man was going to the river for a cruise with friends. Sounded like he'd rather hang with these girls. That proved true. I had a scheduled ride with two other attractive girls. The man insisted I take him and the first set of girls for that pickup. I complied. The next girls got in but were dropped off.

In a nutshell, they were the only people to get out of the car that New Year's night. We kept picking up other riders who also cancelled their plans to stay in the car with others. It went on all night long. They were all dropped off at five in the morning. We went everywhere impulsively. It was a very fun night with complete strangers. They tipped well at the end of the ride in cash.

None of their rides were paid via the ridesharing company. I ended their ride as soon as they agreed to hang out. Use your imagination on where we went and what we did that night. Too many places and I'd rather spare you. It was one of those situations that wouldn't be fun if you weren't there.

That New Year's ride was nearing the end for me. It was a better way to conclude the ridesharing. We did it – like Frank Sinatra used to say – my way.

Future's Uncertain. End is Always Near

The ridesharing was taking its toll. It was one of the most enjoyable experiences there was. The supplemental income and flexibility weren't bad either. What meant the most to me were the experiences and the people. That is something that will never be forgotten or replaced.

Ten thousand rides. Before that, I'd been telling people it was coming to an end. Few people can say they drove 120,000 in a single year. That's a lot of wear and tear on a car. That's a lot of wear and tear on a body sitting in a car that long. I lost track of how many flat tires occurred within those years. It's never fun getting a flat in a bad neighborhood at four in the morning. Didn't help that the newer Prius didn't come with a spare tire.

A tire company often changed or plugged the flats at no cost because I'd frequented their place so often. Free hotdogs, too. It wasn't just that. The riders were starting to irritate me all the time. The fares had been reduced and all kinds of promotions were out there. The ridesharing company was attempting to remain competitive.

Their competitor was attractive. The word on the street was that they paid better and were better to their drivers. I've always been a loyal person to my employers and gave that little consideration. At the end of the day, a ridesharing company was a ridesharing company.

Somebody Else Drive

Twice I offered riders to drive my car. I wanted to kill the app and just tag along for the ride. The first was a girl who'd just passed her driving test. She was excited and her family didn't own a car. The second time was when I picked up a SEPTA bus driver. The road conditions were poor. I was tired. He was complaining about time. "Take the wheel, buddy. I want to see what you got". He laughed and refused but complimented my driving style the entire way. "You'd make a great bus driver". Probably liked my aggressive style. Driving for public transportation was out of the question. Sticking to a real schedule with limited earnings? Not this driver.

Trapped in a Restroom

Have you ever had to go to the bathroom when you're stuck in the middle of center city Philadelphia? I did. It was on Arch Street. There are very few public bathrooms. Let's use that accounting firm's bathroom. It has parking. It's early in the morning. Few employees would be in already.

Of course, the building said, "Employee Entrance Only". I had to go. They reminded me again with a sign that said, "Restrooms are for employees only". Who cares? I had to go. Quick pee and I'd be outta there.

They locked me in the restroom. My phone was left in the car. I banged and banged on the door. A man shouted thru the door "I ain't letting you out. You aren't supposed to be in here".

I pleaded. He didn't care. The other concern was now getting a ticket for being parked in an illegal parking spot out front. I banged and banged. The man "kindly" opened the door and I scurried out without saying a word. Word to the wise: Pay attention to signs. The aftermath isn't always pleasant. The eight hundred block of Arch Street in Philadelphia.

Leaning Tower of Philadelphia

One of the newer and taller buildings in Philadelphia was leaning. Without naming it, let's say it is the building near market. The one close to the train station. It changes colors at night. Two guys took a ride there at one o'clock in the morning. Unusual considering it is an office complex. They were engineers scrambling to figure out a way to get steel up the elevator shafts. The engineers claimed the builders got cheap on the top seven or eight floors. They said the builders used concrete instead of steel.

The men said if they needed to figure it out. The building was going to end up in the Schuylkill river. They named it the leaning tower of Philadelphia. I'd personally would let the building lean. It would give the city a little more character. That's just me.

Dinner Break

Picked a rider up at a mall. Passed right by my house on the way to her destination. She said very little. I wanted to play. Asked her if she minded waiting in the car while I ran into my house for a quick bite to eat. Promised her I would be no longer than an hour.

It was dinner time and my favorite meal was on the table. I was kidding.

The look on the rider's face was priceless. She stuttered, mumbled, but agreed. We went directly to her destination. I never really went into my house. It opened the doors of conversation and made the ride more pleasant. Five stars, baby!

The Car Dealer

One of the best riders I had. He, himself, was also a driver back when he owned a car. Lost a few things along the way to divorce. His house was one of the things he also lost. Got to give him credit for raising the kids alone.

Had the privilege of driving his mother on a few rides. She didn't need to speak highly of her son. The opinion was already formed.

We had several rides together. We always laughed and shared stories. The last time I drove him, he ordered a pizza along the way home. Wanted to pick it up and cruise around all night. I'd have done that with him in a second if I were a single man. We ate the pizza on the hood of the car instead. If anybody's in the market for a Ford, I got a guy.

Woman Power

While driving an addict to rehab, a sensor went off in the car. Could have been anything. Had no clue. Told her I was cutting the ride short. She was in her "working" attire. Really pretty dress.

Under the car she went. The shutter fan was closed. Not sure how that happened but she was quite the mechanic. She performed a forty-point inspection while lying on the ground in her dress. Never underestimate a woman.

Motel McHugh

Busy city. Especially when the Philadelphia Eagles are in the playoffs. Wasn't a hotel availability in the city for a rider on one such occasion. The rider and I checked everywhere. Nothing. She offered to pay me to sleep in my car. She said "Just park it in your driveway. I will be fine and pay you hotel rates". Tempting. Could also have found the car missing in the morning. Didn't happen. Left her at a rest stop on the interstate. Should have charged her hotel rates for suggesting she sleep there. Pretty sure the guards threw her out. I was halfway down the highway when that happened. Home sweet home.

Murals Everywhere

Had the privilege of driving the woman who had the final say on all murals in the city of Philadelphia. Super woman. Message her every once and a while when a new mural goes up in the city. Just my way of letting her know I was thinking about her. Her and most of the riders I've driven. Many times, I'd get separation anxiety after not hearing from a rider. That's what dogs do when their owners leave. I was owned by my riders.

Evolving Market

Ridesharing affected taxi drivers, obviously. It also created a new market. Kids were taking rides to school. They would have never taken a cab. Taxi's just never evolved. A rider didn't always know when they were coming or if they were coming at all.

They never took care of their vehicles. You never knew the fair. Everything changes. Ridesharing may evolve. Ridesharing may disappear. Nothing lasts forever. Had to gram the supplemental money while it was out there.

Bad Gamble

A young immigrant once blew fifty thousand dollars in a single night. Casinos. The only words I could understand as he cried all the way home were fifty thousand dollars. It was hard to feel bad for the guy. This driver didn't even have fifty thousand dollars to gamble with. All I could say to him was "maybe next time".

Liar Liar

Pants on fire. You know, it's crazy how many riders often said they hated liars and thieves. They weren't referring to me or my stories. It was just a common theme when speaking with riders.

I could be wrong but many of them seemed to be the lying themselves. Many of them resembled Pinocchio as the ride went on. I never cared. It was entertaining. Can't say that any of them were thieves but I'm sure there were a few of them, too. I may have exaggerated a few stories on rides, but I never lied. Exaggerating wasn't intentional. Sometimes our minds remember things that never happened. Sometimes our minds unintentionally alter what really happened over time. It made for better tips. Better conversation. Guilty as charged. Be assured, anything written here is verifiable and documented. The sequel may be a different story. Could have a lot of fun releasing a little imagination.

Common Riders

The obvious were riders going to bars. No need to even mention that. Everybody and anybody rode. Nurses were always fun. I'd often joke with them that I wouldn't want to be their patient on the third day of their twelve-hour shift. They'd reply "No, Bill, you don't want to be our patient on the first hour of the first day. Always a good laugh with the nurses.

Students were fun. They keep us young. Once we lose touch with our youth, that begins our aging process. Clerks were fun. Teachers were fun. Construction workers were fun. Everybody was fun. I miss my riders.

Walmart

Now those riders weren't fun. They always had a million bags. It was always in the cold or in the rain and they never tipped. Bags always had to go up a million stairs and the rider had an excuse not to help me carry them. There were times I considered posting a sign on the front of the car that said, "No Walmart Riders".

Tip Net

There were also times I considered slinging a tip net over my left shoulder. While I was driving of course. Makes the ride more entertaining. Couldn't do it. Considered a catch and release scenario. Many riders wouldn't get the humor in begging for a tip then releasing it back to them. The thought just never went away.

Bee Keepers and Hot Dog Carts

Learned how to become a bee keeper from a rider. Was a long two-hour ride. Taught me everything I ever wanted to know about raising bees. The bee population is dying off. The world needs more bee keepers. I could save the world by providing honey. Something to consider after the ridesharing. Pushing a hot dog card along the beach isn't a bad idea, either. Bee sting. Sunburn sting. About the same thing, right? Neither sting could hurt as bad the sting the ridesharing company was putting on anyway.

Lobbyist

Nobody likes those buggers. Except me. They get such a bad rap in the political world. Drove one who was paid to save horses. Apparently, there was a bill passed a few years ago that allowed horses to be exported? They are being captured and deported to Mexico and Canada as a source of food. One day this country may be horseless. Keep the horse lobbyists. They are saving our horses. They other lobbyists? I'd be glad to drive them out of town for you.

Daycare

The rider wasn't just a Daycare worker. She was the president of a bank. Working at her child's daycare was just a part-time passion. She ordered a ride and got a different driver than me. She said "Bill, the guy pulls up and lays on his horn. I tell him I will be out in a minute".

When the rider – one of my favorites – comes out, she can't believe her eyes. There are kids entering the building, kids exiting the building, and her driver. He is peeing up against the wall of the daycare center. He notices her and says "Hey. Hey. You ready"?

I'm laughing as she tells the story and ask her what she did. She said, "I told him to never lay on that horn again". The world isn't crazy. Is it? The president of a bank!

10,000 Maniacs

It was my goal to walk away after ride number ten thousand. It happened kind of accidentally. Two girls were dropped off at a Flyers game. The app was left on all the way up to the point of getting off interstate 95 near home. As I got off the ramp, the traffic light was red. A tractor trailer was stopped at the red light. I stopped behind him. The oncoming driver didn't.

Took a quick glance in the mirror. There was no way to avoid the collision. I remember thinking "Oh, no. I have stuff I didn't get to do. Thought it was the end. Bang! Under the tractor trailer I went. The guy who hit me still had his radio blaring and he also had a pair of earplugs in. He looked like a complete stoner.

Little damage was done to my car. I thought it was totaled. Not a visible scratch anywhere. Amazing. The striking driver said "Sorry. Everything cool? I gotta go". Not that quickly, buddy. I took pictures. We exchanged information. I was willing to let the accident go without even calling the police. Never make that mistake boys and girls.

The following day, it was time for yet another oil change. The hood wouldn't open. Oh no. To the body shop I went. The owner said, "This car may be totaled". What? He said if he forced the hood to open, we may not get it closed again. The frame could be damaged. He was correct. On ride number ten thousand, the damages totaled ten thousand. Coincidental.

I should have settled for 9,999 rides and walked away. I was that tired of driving. The car went into the shop for what would be forty-two days. Martin Luther King Day was the following day. The ridesharing company would be closed. There was some unfinished business with them as well. I wanted my final bonus.

Show Me More Money

The ridesharing company often had incentives. They were hard to reach working a full-time job. That was causing undue stress. I needed to hit a hundred rides to get an eighty-dollar bonus for the week. I managed. I mean I would have managed. A glitch in their system ruined my cornflakes. They accidentally disabled my app. Said I exceeded my driving time. Impossible! I drove a total of two hours on that day. The only driving time I exceeded was driving for that ridesharing company.

Before I quit, I wanted that bonus. It was owed to me. The trip to the company would be a time killer. Sat there several hours. When called to the counter, I reviewed the driving time. The counter boy took another hour to sift through the trips. He couldn't find it anywhere. While waiting, I received an email from the company that a rider didn't like my driving style.

Shocking. My ratings for most of my career were the highest in the state of Pennsylvania. There were never complaints. Sent them a brief email back saying that I was currently at their hub. I wasn't happy about being shorted bonus money. I then brought the email to the clerk's attention. "Impossible", he stated. I don't see anything. Another email. This one said that there were several complaints over the last two weeks. They said I was notified via email, on the app, and via phone call. Impossible. I freaked out on the clerk. "What is going on, here", he asked. We were both puzzled.

He was a supervisor. He then huddled with other supervisors. Upon returning, he stated there was a glitch in their software but couldn't pay the bonus. This driver got a tad temperamental but maintained his cool. "I want my money. Your software glitch is not my problem". They huddled again. He came back and said they were going to pay the bonus.

"What about those complaints", I asked. "They must have been a glitch as well", he replied. "Don't worry about it. Nothing is showing anywhere. You have the highest ratings I've ever seen", he stated. Fact is, there were no complaints.

It's Over

Ridesharing company it's over. Your baby doesn't love you any-more. I must admit, I went a little unprofessional upon exiting. They wasted my time in their office all day. Their attitudes were terrible. My bad hair day. I began snapping pictures of my perfect ratings. It showed zero complaints from their electronic board. I was also making a few unprofessional remarks but nothing note-worthy. It was at that time, I said "if I don't get my bonus money, my lawyer will get if for me". The dwarfs weren't happy. They were more like Dopy and Snow White was nowhere to be found when summoned.

The supervisor summons five security guards instead. "He men-tioned lawyers. We can't deal with him anymore", one stated. I snapped more pictures of the perfect ratings. Those guards de-manded my phone and the pictures that were on it. There were two hundred people watching this at their hub. I was ready to rumble with the guards. They weren't getting my phone. "For your protection, you guys better call the police", I barked. They backed off. I left the building.

Can you believe when I got out to my car, the app was disabled? I stormed back in. We argued some more. People were starring. It wasn't worth anymore words. I was done driving anyway. It was over. There were other supplemental opportunities with their competitor. That wasn't going to happen. I remembered wanting to be done with the ridesharing for other reasons. Besides, my car went into the shop for body damage. I couldn't drive for them or anybody else, anyway. They do not allow drivers to use rental cars. Good time to step back and smell the roses.

Somebody That I Used to Know

Mimi is my mom's nickname. That has nothing to do with the price of tea in China. Just saying. It's also the nickname of a rider never mentioned. That's partially out of respect for her. It's also because nothing unusual ever happened that would appeal to a reader. But his woman made a difference. She became my eyes and ears in Kensington.

Mimi obviously had struggles. She was one of the first people I met in Kensington. One night, she was "working" the corner. It was raining and cold. Slow night for both of us. I knew her deal. She knew I was doing ridesharing. I offered to get her out of the rain for a few minutes and to talk. We went down the road to an Arby's for a little ice cream. She liked rice pudding.

We had so many talks. Mimi never asked me for anything. I never asked her for anything. Ever. There were a lot of attempts to get her into rehab.

Mimi once said, "You like helping us. It makes you feel better about yourself". That was a upsetting remark, but it was correct. She went on to say, "You help us because we make your issues look small". Also upsetting. Also correct. A professional therapist couldn't have said it better. We kept it real with each other and we both appreciated honest facts.

Without Mimi protecting me from other addicts, things would have taken a bad turn. Nobody messed with her. We were honest with each other. We respected each other. Mimi was my friend.

Mimi was the first person that I took to my house. It got her off the street. We'd talk. She'd make a lot of peanut butter and jelly sandwiches. Mimi protected me from the other addicts. Things would have taken a bad turn. Nobody messed with her. We were honest with each other. We respected each other.

Tusk

Tusk is one of my favorite songs. My favorite version had over one hundred drummers. It didn't include my favorite band member Lindsey Buckingham. He disagreed with the song and the meaning of the song. Tusk is slang for Penis.

Why don't you ask him if he's going to stay? Why don't you ask him if he's going away? The lyrics applied to the girls in Kensington. Everybody promised them the world. Many offered them help. Many had hidden agendas.

The girls burned their share of men and the men burned their share of girls. It wasn't only about drugs. It was also about the tusk. It's a vicious cycle. Good intentions? Probably. Poor implementation? Definitely. Both men and women were looking for love in all the wrong places. "Just tell me that you love me".

As tempting as some of the girls were, I never violated any of them. Many people did. They may have manipulated a lot of men, but they were still somebody's daughter. Somebody's mother. Mimi was somebody's mother. Mimi was somebody's daughter.

Rice Pudding

One night, Mimi was dope sick. I had a few other addicts in the car that were also going to rehab. None of them could do their drugs in my car. I never allowed that. Mimi was sick. Really sick. I'd offered her five dollars to get well. "Stop the car, Mother Bleeper", she shouted. "I will blankety blank a blankety blank before I EVER take a nickel from you", she continued. She jumped out - as sick as she was - to find money elsewhere. That's the kind of respect she had for me. I made the other girls wait until she did her thing. That's the kind of respect I had for her. There was no way I was leaving Mimi on the streets of Kensington.

The others were important. Mimi was – and always will be – number one. Sincerity and honesty don't exist on the streets of Kensington. With Mimi, it did.

Mimi is doing well now. We remain friends from a distance. She is recovering, living on her own, and is another person who will live the good life that she deserves. Mimi, I see a rice pudding in our future one day. I Miss you, my friend. Keep doing what you're doing.

Oh, By the Way

You've heard a few tales of ridesharing events. You've also heard some encounters with addicts who've struggled. This past October – October 5, 2018 to be exact – a friend from grade school messaged me on Facebook.

"You've worked with a lot of addicts. Have you seen this girl? She may have made her way to Kensington". It was a picture of a red-headed woman who appeared to be in her early thirties. She was exceptionally pretty. That's always the ones.

OMG! I recognized the girl. She was the last rider of the night towards the end of June. That post had gotten over forty-four thousand shares on Facebook. It was posted by the missing girl's sister in California. She was pleading for people to help her find her missing sister. That post made its way across the country.

That night in June, the girl had multiple stops on her trip when I picked her up. It was 2:30 in the morning. The first stop was to Chester. Lovely drug ridden neighborhood. The girl was as professional as anybody. The conversation was great. She was going to pay her landlord. At two thirty in the morning? Whatever.

When we reached the house, the girl said "park up and kill the lights. Holy...I knew what that meant. This girl didn't fit the image. I knew what she was doing. I asked the girl if she needed any help. She said, "It's not doing what you think. I worked all night as a waitress and this was the only chance to pay the rent". Yeah, okay. I did my job but refused to kill the lights.

The girl had other stops afterwards. Three of them to be exact. Along the way, I talked about many struggling addicts I'd encountered. The woman wasn't listening and didn't care. I dropped her off at a hotel in Chester at the end of her rides.

When the childhood friend sent me the picture, I immediately went to the police station. The police station in the town where I picked the woman up in June. The officers noted the details of the ride and said they would be in touch. They reached out to the girl's mother.

The woman was found three hours later. She had been missing for more than five weeks. It was a good feeling to be standing in her living room hugging her. The girl had been held captive in the basement of a seedy hotel in Chester. That was one of the stops along our trip that night.

Boys and girls, you can't make this stuff up! All those months that went by since that ride in June. The ties the woman had to prominent people won't be mentioned. It's a little too crazy for one to believe.

Song Bird

Standing in the line to see the show tonight and there's a light on, heavy glow. By the way I tried to say I'd be there. Waiting for you.

It was funeral. Nicole's funeral. I wanted to be there for her. Offered to be waiting for a dozen others who passed during my ridesharing days. Waiting when they were ready for rehab.

I always wanted to help them. Nicole used to help me help others. She used to meet me on the Eastside in the city where the sun doesn't set. She used to meet me on the Eastside. She used to meet me on the Eastside.

I'm sorry that I let you down. All these voices in my head get loud. I'm sorry that I let you down. Let you down.

Tell me something, boy. Aren't you tired tryin' to fill that void? Or do you need more?
It's hard keeping it so hardcore. In all the good times I find myself longing for change. And in the bad times I fear myself.

Brother from Another Mother

I have a friend who can tell you the score of all the local sports teams. He can go back over twenty years. Try to hold a normal conversation with him and it's a different story. He's all over the place. Other friends say we are very similar. He remembers scores. I remember rides.

I used to joke with people that I could remember every single rider of the 10,000 rides. Maybe that's an exaggeration. Maybe it's true. Some people can remember every actor and actress in a movie. It's been a good number of years since I've seen a movie. There's no need to. My riders have given me a memory to last a lifetime.

Your friends are the ones who Lyft you up when nobody else noticed you fall. Lyft is a ridesharing competitor. They knew I still had the urge to drive. How was that possible? I told all my friends I never wanted to drive for a ridesharing company again. They texted me their promo code anyway. They knew. Same stuff. Different day. Wasn't happening.

Side Note Review

"You're quite the writer, aren't you, McHugh"? That's a quote from a person who has had a lot of rides in the Toyota Prius. I sent her over a few paragraphs to read that were about her. She's lucky she even got to know my last name with all the struggles we had.

There was sarcasm in her response. One of the things I always liked about her. She isn't getting any royalties if there are any. I was smart enough not to name her. She will know who she is, though. Her last comment on a recent post was "Shut the freak up. I can't even take you serious half the time". Correct. And I like it that way.

One of the other "crazies" was also asked to read a section of the stories. She breaks my heart. Her eyes are always far away. Her spoken words are lonely. She didn't care if I used her real name.

Royalties would do her no good anyway. Her life is going to be short. I's inevitable. Oh, how I would like to be wrong this time. It's so sad. A woman with every reason to who just can't get her life straight. There are so many people like her. Really, it's all of us to some degree.

Goodbye Strangers

It was an early morning yesterday. I was up before the dawn. And I really have enjoyed my stay. But I must be moving on. Goodbye Mary. Goodbye Jane. Feel no sorrow. Feel no shame. Come tomorrow. Feel no pain.

Never Give Up

Working in challenged areas with challenged people helped me become a better person. I appreciate life and understand the struggles of others. I had learned to listen to people's emotions and their tone of voice. No longer did I only hear their language and accents. I heard their sorrow. I heard their laughter. I heard their emotions.

Ridesharing isn't for everybody although, I'd recommend everybody give it a shot. It's good supplemental income. It's risky at times. Drivers struggle with riders. Riders struggle with drivers. Whichever you are, never give up. Don't become anybody's breakfast. Simply, grab them by the throat before they swallow you.

Me? I was never a driver for a ridesharing company. I, indeed, was a just a passenger in the lives of others.

Made in the USA
Middletown, DE
12 July 2019